# Garden Magic

Ann Taylor

**Garden Magic**
Ann Taylor



This edition published in Great Britain 2004 by
The Windsor Group
The Old School House,
St John's Court,
Moulsham Street,
Chelmsford,
Essex CM2 OJD

**ISBN 1-903904-43-9**

Typeset by SJ Design and Publishing, Bromley, Kent



Note: The contents of this book have been carefully checked for accuracy. Readers are advised that they should not take for granted to use of new formulas or mixtures and that they should always seek advice from horticulturists and manufacturers before embarking on new methods of horticulture. Neither the author nor the publisher can accept legal responsibility for any problems that may arise out of experimentation with any of the methods, recommendations or suggestions described in this book.

# Introduction

Have you ever noticed how some gardens always look good even though their owners seem to spend less time than you tending their plants? Chances are they have discovered the many secrets of successful gardening known only to a handful of lucky people, secrets that are divulged for you now in *Garden Magic*.

This book is the culmination of 50 years of hands-on experience making gardening into an easy, successful, low-cost hobby using common household items in preference to costly proprietary brands.

The result is staggering – yes, truly staggering! You will suddenly find the hours spent in your garden are fewer, less arduous, and immensely more pleasurable than you ever thought possible. Gardening – and the fruits of your labours – should be enjoyed, and not be a source of constant pain and worry.

We hope you enjoy reading *Garden Magic* as well as practising its message in your garden.

Good luck.

**Ann Taylor**

# Contents

SECTION 1

# Lawns

Planting one of the more hardy grasses can help keep your lawn in shape and green through the summer and helps to maintain a green appearance during spring, autumn, and winter seasons. The days when lawns had to be weed-free are long gone. Nowadays, if you prefer, you can allow the grass to grow longer, or keep it short, there are no hard and fast rules. If you wish you can be a perfectionist, nurturing grass into a faultless green sward that will be the envy of your neighbours.

When starting a new lawn you can choose to raise it from grass seed, or lay it as turf. Both methods produce excellent results, but turf is almost instant, whereas seed takes a full season to reach perfection. Seed is the cheaper option, especially for large areas to be put to lawn; it also gives a wider choice of grass types. For a small garden lawn, turfing is by far the easier option, and can be laid at any time of the year, but spring or autumn are the best times.

## PREPARATION

Dig over the area that is to become your new lawn. Use a rotavator if you have a large area to prepare. Remove all rubble, large stones, weeds, and old tree roots. Make sure that the ground drains freely. If the soil is poor, add a layer of about 10cm of topsoil mixed, if possible, with peat-free soil-enriched compost. Rake over, and level the site.

Firm down the soil, either by rolling with a heavy roller, or by treading the entire area with your feet. Rake over again, and repeat the firming and raking process until the whole site is level, even and firm. Scratch over the site one last time leaving about 5cm of tilth on the surface.

Before laying turf consider sprinkling a good fertiliser, about 50g per square metre, to give the grass roots a good start. When buying the turf, measure the area of the intended lawn and add an extra square metre to ensure that you have enough to cover the whole area. Plan to lay the turf as soon as it is delivered to prevent it deteriorating. If that isn't possible, unroll the turf, so that the grass receives the light of day.

When buying seed, consider first the location of the site. There are seed mixtures suitable for shady gardens as well as for lawns that are going to be used as play areas, or just for general purposes. You will find the recommended sowing rate on the packaging when you buy your seed. Don't worry about being precise when sowing; the wind and rain will ensure that the seed is well dispersed over the site. Any disparity of germination will soon put itself right within the first season of growth.

Choose a calm, dry day for sowing seed, and then after sowing lightly rake the seed into the soil. A small lawn may be tamped down by laying a plank over the seeded ground and then firmed with your own weight, by treading end to end on the plank to flatten the ground. A large site will need to be rolled with a light roller. If the weather remains dry for more than 24 hours after sowing, apply a fine spray of water to the area.

Keep off the lawn until it is established and ready for the first cut, which should be a gentle topping of the grass to encourage basal side shoots. Thereafter mow your lawn once a week.

A good, properly maintained mower is essential for any lawn, but outlay can be high so you must choose a mower that suits your lawn best. Various models suit different kinds of lawn and some will be highly unsuitable for individual requirements. A lightweight electric mower is useless for bumpy lawns with rough grass and thick weeds. In cases like this, a rotary petrol mower is usually best.

The following guidelines will help you decide on a model to suit your lawn, but always check first to be sure the mower can cope with peculiarities, like rough grass, proximity to concrete walls, and so on.

**Small Lawn**
Less than 50 square metres: electric mower with cutting width of 25-30cm.

**Medium Lawn**
Between 50-275 square metres: petrol mower with cutting width of 30-35cm.

**Large Lawn**
Over 275 square metres: self-propelled mower with grass collector and cutting width of 35-45cm.

Grass, like all plants, needs food. Constant mowing leaves it particularly under nourished. Feed at least twice a year with a good lawn fertiliser that is high in nitrogen, to help the grass withstand wear and tear and dry spells. Aim to apply fertilisers before light rain is expected, and never during a dry spell. Don't be tempted to increase the amount of fertiliser more than the recommended measure, as the grass will burn and turn brown.

## TIPS

### 1. Should I buy ordinary grass seed?

Well-manicured lawns are largely down to sowing the best grass seeds and careful tending. Many seeds from garden centres and nurseries are past their sell-by date, even though it's often hard to tell. Always check with the experts first and ask for the latest supplies of grass seeds they have. Always check the delivery or sell-by date, if available.

**2. How do I stop birds from eating newly-sown seed?**
Seed-eating birds are a problem on all unprotected, newly-sown lawns. Small nets, supported on stakes driven into the ground are the best protective devices for small lawns. Larger lawns can be protected with strips of bright plastic or bunches of feathers or white rags, tied to string and fastened to stakes driven into the lawn at regular intervals. Black thread, criss-crossed in a maze across the lawn a few centimetres from the surface is a very good way to deter birds. Bear in mind that sparrows and some other small birds quickly become accustomed to any obstacle, so that, after a short time, it is essential to apply another device to deter them.

**3. How often should I mow my lawn?**
All lawns, new or long established, need to be mown often to stop them becoming ragged. In very hot weather, the grass must not be cut too close, or the roots may be scorched.

**4. What is the best method of mowing a lawn?**
Mowing is best done in alternate directions, the mower being pushed along the length of the lawn on one day, and across the width the next time you mow. Rolling should be done in the same fashion. If not, the lawn develops a wavy appearance.

**5. Is it beneficial to sweep a lawn?**
Sweeping the lawn is a worthwhile deterrent, discouraging the growth of moss and distributing worm casts, while at the same time removing any unsightliness and spreading an excellent top-dressing of fine soil over the grass.

**6. How do I aerate my lawn?**
To keep your lawn in top condition, regularly make small punctures in the topsoil to let the air circulate and help drainage. An electric lawn-rake makes the job easier and can be hired from most garden centres and nurseries.

**7. My lawn looks bare in places, what can I do about it?**
An old lawn may have bare spots that need replanting. Try renovating the lawn or installing a new one with some of the newer turf grass cultivars that have been bred for disease and wear resistance, slower growth, and drought tolerance. Look for mixtures that include perennial rye grass varieties.

**8. How should I dispose of leaves and grass cuttings?**
Rake and gather fallen leaves to add to your compost pile. Also add the grass cuttings to your compost.

**9. Will fallen leaves harm my lawn in the winter months?**
Do not let fallen leaves cover your lawn during winter. This covering robs the lawn of the air it needs to regenerate itself for the coming season.

**10. Is it true that soot is a good bird repellent?**
Yes, you can keep birds away from your newly-seeded lawn by dusting the area with soot. Birds hate soot. However, remember that rain destroys the effect so you will need to replace the soot after every shower.

**11. My lawn is full of ant nests, what can I do?**
Get rid of ants quickly and inexpensively. Inverted plant-pots make excellent exterminators. Cover the hole in the bottom of the pot and place it upside down over the ant nest. Pour cold water around the rim every day. After a few days, part of the nest will transfer to the pot under which you can slip a square of cardboard or plastic and remove the nest. To destroy the nest, drop it in a dish of salted water.

**12. How can I eradicate clover from my lawn?**
Remove clover from the lawn by sprinkling nitrate of soda over the affected areas. Rake the lawn first and apply about 3g of nitrate to every square metre.

**13. How can I eradicate moss from my lawn?**
Remove moss from grassy areas by sprinkling with bone-meal after you have raked the moss out first.

**14. My lawn is infested with worms; how can I reduce their numbers?**
Banish worms from the lawn by soaking with a mixture of 3g of slaked lime to a litre of warm water for every square metre that you treat.

**15. How do I level an established lawn?**
Bumps or hollows are dealt with by cutting the affected turf along three sides, leaving the fourth to serve as a kind of hinge. The turf, cut through below, is rolled back and soil either taken away or added, as required. Roll back the top and beat into place with the back of a spade or a well-aimed heel.

**16. How can I tell if there are hollows in my lawn?**
Lawn unevenness are more easily detected by setting a plank on the turf, on edge, getting someone to hold it in place, then going down on one's hands and knees some distance away and peering beneath the plank to spot the gaps.

**17. How do I renovate a worn lawn?**
When turfing cannot repair patches in the lawn, the crust of old, bare soil can be broken down with a garden fork and the soil turned over to about 15cm deep. Firm the ground and plant with seed at the rate of about 3g to every square metre. Cover with sifted soil and press down hard. Take precautions to keep birds at bay.

**18. How do I get rid of weeds in my lawn?**
During spring and summer, vigorous and regular sweeping with a stout brush can remove annual weeds. In winter, the weeds can be raked off with a really sharp rake. After treatment, the lawn will appear to be entirely ruined; but it is not, especially if more grass seed is sown at the rate of 3g per square metre (or less if the lawn is not badly damaged).

**19. Is walking on a frozen lawn bad for the grass?**
Avoid walking on turf when it's frozen, as it will damage the grass. Wait until the turf is completely defrosted.

**20. What is the best method of getting rid of perennial weeds?**
Daisies can be removed with a knife or grubber. Dipping an iron skewer in strong carbolic or sulphuric acid or weed-killer, and then plunging it straight down into the crown should kill off plantains, thistles, and other deep-rooted weeds. Many smaller weeds can be destroyed by giving the turf a dressing of lawn sand in the early spring. Lawn sand poisons daisies and other weeds and stimulates the grass. It often makes the grass look black to start with, but the colour quickly returns.

**21. How should I lay-up my motor mower for the winter?**
If you've finished mowing for the season, run the engine dry and remove the spark plug. Pour 2 tablespoonfuls of engine oil into the cylinder and crank the engine a few times to prevent the cylinder from rusting. Change the oil while the engine is still warm and clean or replace the air and oil filters.

**22. I have been told that I can use slaked lime on my lawn. Is this true?**

Well-slaked lime, old soot, burnt wood, vegetable peelings and ashes make wonderful foodstuffs for grassy and lawn areas. Sieve everything well before sprinkling on the surface.

## HOME RECIPES FOR LAWN TREATMENTS

### Spring Treatment for Lawns

*Ingredients:*

1 tbsp washing-up liquid or children's shampoo
1 tbsp antiseptic mouthwash

*Method:*

Combine ingredients in a 5-litre hose sprayer. Top up with water then spray over the lawn. Quantity is sufficient for small- to medium-sized lawns. For larger lawns, increase the measurements accordingly.

### All-Year-Round Lawn Food

Dry food is best during the spring.

Add 1.5kg Epsom salts to every 25kg dry fertiliser mix. Apply half the recommended amount for the fertiliser using a hand-held spreader on a medium setting. Two days later, spray liberally with Super Lawn Tonic (see below).

### Super Lawn Tonic

*Ingredients:*

1 can of beer
1 tbsp washing-up liquid

*Method:*

Mix the ingredients in a 5-litre hose sprayer.

**All-Season Lawn Disease Tonic**
*Ingredients:*
1 can of beer
1 can of cola
1 tbsp washing-up liquid
1 tbsp antiseptic mouthwash
$^{1}/_{4}$ tsp instant tea granules
*Method:*
Combine ingredients in a 5-litre hose sprayer. Spray liberally on the lawn.

**Autumn Lawn Weed-Killer**
Start by diluting 1 tablespoonful of washing-up liquid in a 5-litre hose sprayer filled with warm water. Add the recommended amount of weed-killer to liquid ratio and spray liberally on your lawn.

**Autumn Special Lawn Feed**
*Ingredients:*
1.5kg Epsom salts
25kg fertiliser
*Method:*
Combine ingredients and apply half the recommended amount for your lawn size using a hand-held broadcast spreader on a medium setting.

**Autumn Follow-Up Lawn Tonic**
Two weeks after treating with Autumn Special Lawn Feed, over-spray with a mixture of 1 can of beer and 1 tablespoonful of washing-up liquid added to a 5-litre hose sprayer.

**Home-Made Lawn Fertiliser**
To make 5 litres:
*Ingredients:*
1 tbsp Epsom salts

25ml household ammonia
Water
*Method:*
Combine the Epsom salts and ammonia in a clean jar. To use, mix 2 tablespoonfuls of the mixture with 5 litres of water in a watering-can and sprinkle on the grass or turf. This is enough for 50 square metres of ground area. To use with a hose attachment, pour the liquid into a sprayer unit.

**All-Season Lawn Tonic**
*Ingredients:*
1 can beer
1 tbsp ammonia
$^{1}/_{2}$ cup of liquid lawn food
$^{1}/_{2}$ cup of molasses
*Method:*
Combine ingredients in a 5-litre hose sprayer and apply to the lawn every three weeks or so.

**Insect Control Tonic**
*Ingredients:*
1 cup washing-up liquid
1 cup chewing tobacco juice
1 cup antiseptic mouthwash
*Method:*
Combine ingredients in a 5-litre hose sprayer topped up with warm water.

## Section 2

# The Flower Garden

Most bedding plants prefer an open, sunny site protected from strong winds. To achieve the best colour displays, wait until the danger of frost has passed before planting out in the garden. Dig over the soil and fork in composted bark and good organic compost to give good drainage. Add to the compost a dressing of fertiliser such as 'Growmore' to give adequate nutrients. Slow-release fertilisers are excellent for flower-beds because they give the plants an even supply of nutrients throughout the growing season. Always follow the manufacturer's recommendations when applying fertiliser and you won't go far wrong.

When planting up your flower garden, plant shrubs first, so that they will be in their permanent quarters, and can remain undisturbed by other planting around them. Give shrubs plenty of space in between to allow them to grow to their full size. Next, plant the perennials. These are the plants that will flower every year, and will be the mainstay of your flowering plants each year. Then plant your annuals in between the shrubs and perennials to give you that extra colour during the summer months. When planting a border, place the tallest plants at the back, and the shortest in the front. After planting, apply about 10cm of mulch on the surface of the soil to conserve moisture and to prevent weeds. Finally, water thoroughly. A liquid fertiliser can be applied with the water when planting to provide some immediate nutrients.

## TIPS

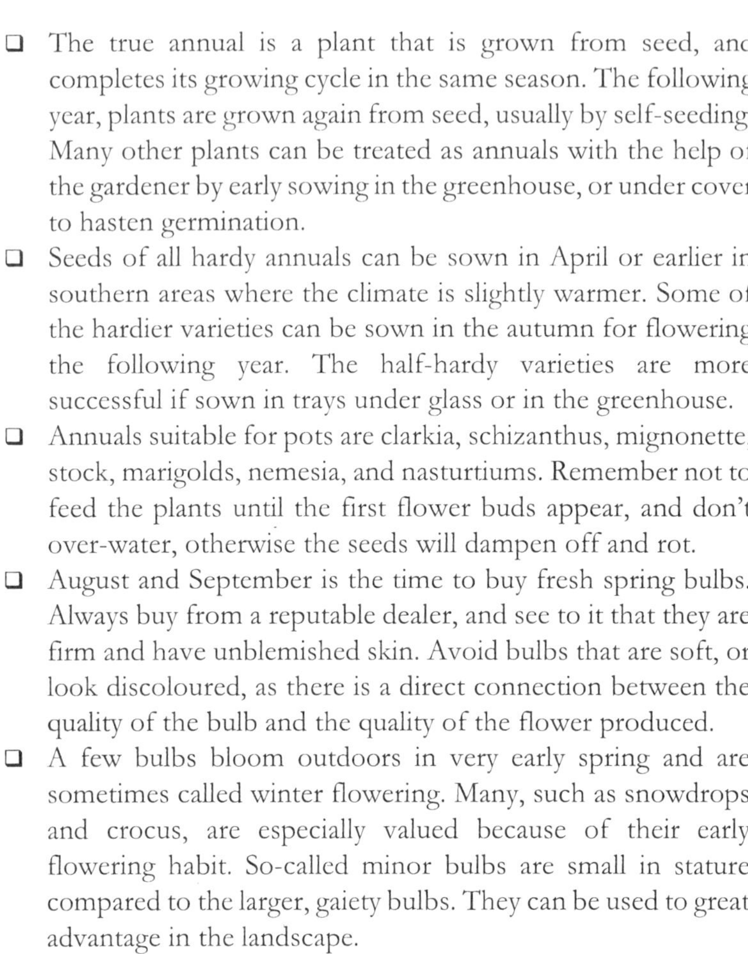

- ❑ The true annual is a plant that is grown from seed, and completes its growing cycle in the same season. The following year, plants are grown again from seed, usually by self-seeding. Many other plants can be treated as annuals with the help of the gardener by early sowing in the greenhouse, or under cover to hasten germination.
- ❑ Seeds of all hardy annuals can be sown in April or earlier in southern areas where the climate is slightly warmer. Some of the hardier varieties can be sown in the autumn for flowering the following year. The half-hardy varieties are more successful if sown in trays under glass or in the greenhouse.
- ❑ Annuals suitable for pots are clarkia, schizanthus, mignonette, stock, marigolds, nemesia, and nasturtiums. Remember not to feed the plants until the first flower buds appear, and don't over-water, otherwise the seeds will dampen off and rot.
- ❑ August and September is the time to buy fresh spring bulbs. Always buy from a reputable dealer, and see to it that they are firm and have unblemished skin. Avoid bulbs that are soft, or look discoloured, as there is a direct connection between the quality of the bulb and the quality of the flower produced.
- ❑ A few bulbs bloom outdoors in very early spring and are sometimes called winter flowering. Many, such as snowdrops and crocus, are especially valued because of their early flowering habit. So-called minor bulbs are small in stature compared to the larger, gaiety bulbs. They can be used to great advantage in the landscape.
- ❑ Plant bulbs in groups of five to ten bulbs, depending on their size, in large pots, and keep them in a cool place in the potting shed away from direct daylight. By late autumn the roots will have formed, and the bulbs will be ready to plant out.
- ❑ Instead of disturbing bulb roots when planting out, by taking them out of their pots, place your bulbs, still in their pots into

the ground where you want them to grow. Cover each pot with soil to a depth of about 5cm, being careful to make sure there are no air pockets around the pot. Within a few months, your bulbs will be sprouting, ready to give you a colourful spring display. Once the blooms have gone over, you can take the bulbs out of their pots and plant them directly into the ground, or dry them off in your potting shed, and save them for another display of colour next year.

- ❑ To mark areas where there are underlying bulbs (tulips, for example) cut out the centre of a coffee jar lid and put the outside rim over the foliage as it dies back. Press it into the top of the soil but be sure not to push it too hard or it won't be visible. You will then know where the bulbs are, and won't accidentally dig them up when planting annuals.
- ❑ Most spring-flowering bulbs prefer light shade to full sunshine. Try to select a site that provides at least six to ten hours of dappled sunlight per day. Light requirements for other bulbs, especially the summer bulbs, are more variable. Select a spot where they will receive the recommended amount of light for the species that you are planting. Insufficient light usually results in poor flowering, but too much light will bleach the flowers and foliage of some species.
- ❑ When selecting previous seasons bulbs for replanting, discard any bulbs that show any sign of disease.
- ❑ Bulbs are generally graded and sold according to size. Large bulbs produce larger and/or multiple flowers. The largest bulbs are not necessary for good landscape effect. In most cases, medium grades are entirely satisfactory.
- ❑ If you want an annual flower such as larkspur, poppies, or balsam to self-sow in your garden, plan ahead so you will recognise the seedlings when they emerge next spring. Take a good long look at the foliage on the mature plants so you are familiar with it. You can also consult a reference book or take pictures to spot them next spring.

- Strong sunlight and drying winds may do as much harm as cold days and nights. Carry portable container-grown tender plants to sheltered sites or indoors. Reduce watering and feeding to frost-tender plants to give them a period of rest. Leave hardy plants outside. Protect the roots by sinking containers up to the rim in a hole in the ground and packing sand between the soil and the pot. Alternatively, surround the plant with mulch or cover with meadow hay. Continue watering throughout the winter on mild days, or whenever the soil in pots isn't frozen and can absorb water.
- If you don't have the space for a regular garden, consider building a permanent raised-bed garden. Using materials such as blocks, bricks, rocks, or wood, construct raised beds at least 10cm tall, one metre wide, and as long as you wish. The height can be shorter if built on top of soil or gravel, but must be at least 10cm tall if built on asphalt or concrete. Fill the inside of the bed with a mixture of garden soil and compost and start planting.
- Since shasta daisies spread very quickly, plant divisions inside a plastic container that has the bottom removed. That way the spreading is minimised to a much more desirable size.
- Start California poppies early indoors to provide an early display of blooms.
- Pinch back petunias' new growth to encourage bushiness rather than 'leggy' plants.
- When first planting, water on a daily basis. If you water too much though, plants might suffer due to over-watering.
- When building a new flower-bed over a grassy area, mow the grass short; cover the area with landscape fabric or plastic, then a thick layer of organic mulch. By the second season, the grass will have rotted and the ground will be ready for planting.
- Watering at night can cause mildew on plants and flowers. Try doing your watering in the morning, and try to keep the moisture away from the foliage.

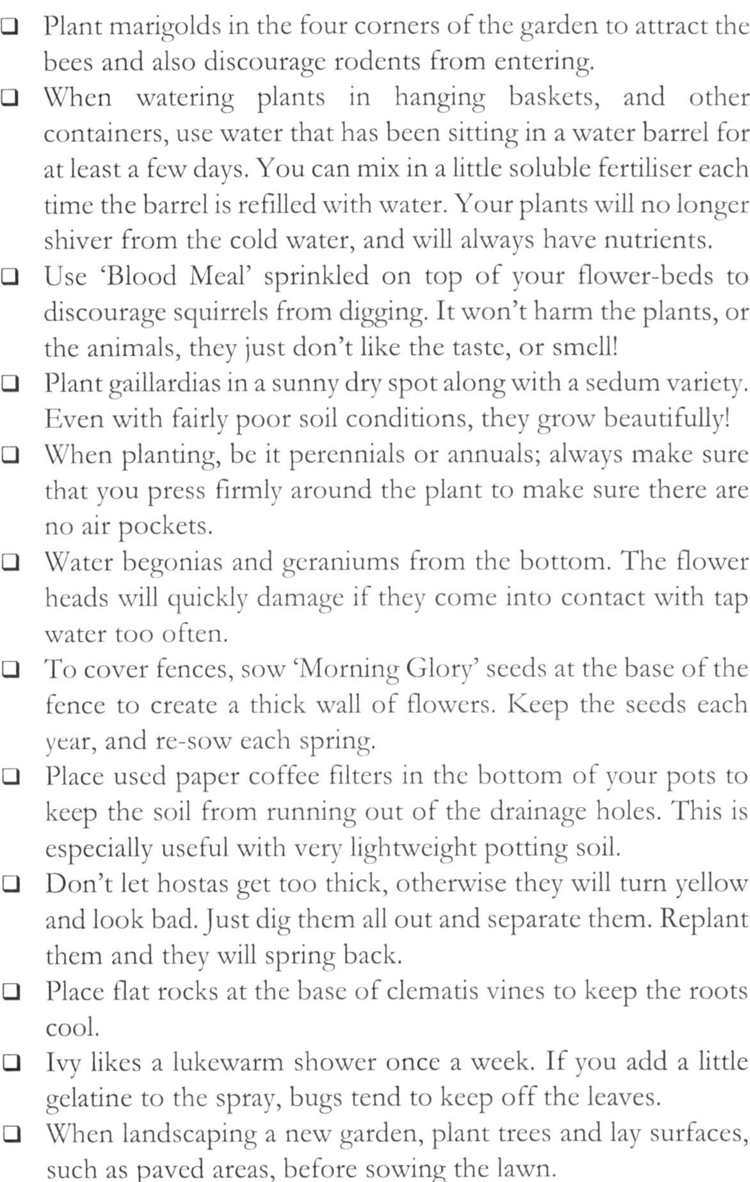

- Plant marigolds in the four corners of the garden to attract the bees and also discourage rodents from entering.
- When watering plants in hanging baskets, and other containers, use water that has been sitting in a water barrel for at least a few days. You can mix in a little soluble fertiliser each time the barrel is refilled with water. Your plants will no longer shiver from the cold water, and will always have nutrients.
- Use 'Blood Meal' sprinkled on top of your flower-beds to discourage squirrels from digging. It won't harm the plants, or the animals, they just don't like the taste, or smell!
- Plant gaillardias in a sunny dry spot along with a sedum variety. Even with fairly poor soil conditions, they grow beautifully!
- When planting, be it perennials or annuals; always make sure that you press firmly around the plant to make sure there are no air pockets.
- Water begonias and geraniums from the bottom. The flower heads will quickly damage if they come into contact with tap water too often.
- To cover fences, sow 'Morning Glory' seeds at the base of the fence to create a thick wall of flowers. Keep the seeds each year, and re-sow each spring.
- Place used paper coffee filters in the bottom of your pots to keep the soil from running out of the drainage holes. This is especially useful with very lightweight potting soil.
- Don't let hostas get too thick, otherwise they will turn yellow and look bad. Just dig them all out and separate them. Replant them and they will spring back.
- Place flat rocks at the base of clematis vines to keep the roots cool.
- Ivy likes a lukewarm shower once a week. If you add a little gelatine to the spray, bugs tend to keep off the leaves.
- When landscaping a new garden, plant trees and lay surfaces, such as paved areas, before sowing the lawn.

- Plant asparagus, fern and ivy in hanging baskets with annuals. After the annuals have finished blooming, you will still have the greenery in your baskets.
- When putting plants, shrubs or small trees into a container to be transplanted later, line the bottom and sides with a mesh made out of nylon or something that approximates the mesh bag that onions and other vegetables come in. Then it is easier to just lift out the mesh and your plants will come out freely, without having to knock on the pot or tip it, which may disturb the roots.
- Clematis need at least three years to get their roots established before they begin to flower well. Those that require sunshine really do need sun for the good part of the day to flower. The foliage will be green and full, but flowers come from the warmth of the sun. They also do well with mulching and a good amount of water at their base. They like their feet cool and their faces hot!
- To help support tall annuals and perennials, keep them from falling over by placing a cage over the plants while they are still small.
- If you are landscaping your own garden, keep in mind the contrasts between plants, house, or any other building beside it.
- Always place the tallest plants in the back of your garden, working your way down. For example: If you plant a 2-metre high shrub in the back, you may want your next plant in front of it to be around 1.5 metres high, and work down by 0.75 metres.
- When planting easy annuals like petunias and marigolds, pinch off any blooms that come on the plants. This encourages much more in new growth that couldn't be accomplished in the nursery packs.
- If you buy plants before you have had a chance to prepare your beds for planting, be ready to protect the plants until planting

time. Protect plants from drying by placing them in a partially shaded area protected from drying winds. Most nursery plants will dry out rapidly. Look at them each day and water them as needed. If it will be more than three or four days before you can begin planting, you need to provide additional protection for the roots. Cluster the plants close together and mulch the roots with compost, straw or rotted sawdust. This will help keep the plants moist until planting.

- ❑ When buying new plants, leave the label on after planting until you have memorised its common and botanical name as well as its location in the garden. You can then take off the label and save it in your gardening diary for future reference.
- ❑ When transplanting day lilies that are still in flower cut the stems and leaves off into a fan just like you would with irises. This allows the plant to concentrate on establishing root growth rather than on blooms.
- ❑ Plant variegated dogwood shrubs in areas that can sometimes receive too much water, and sometimes not enough, that is to say, under eaves, or by rainspouts. They thrive with the extra watering, but like to be dry, too.
- ❑ Try to get a variety of flowers that bloom at different times of the year, so that you always have flowers in your garden to give colour.
- ❑ When you start your seedlings, cut up little strips of plastic and line your pots with about 5cm hanging over either side. When you are ready to pop out the seedlings, pull the strips up. This way you won't end up tearing the seedlings from their roots.
- ❑ Store unused seeds in a refrigerator in airtight containers, mixed with a few tablespoonfuls of dried milk powder.
- ❑ Maximise your lighting for seedlings, by adding a strip of aluminium foil to each side of the seed box. Make sure you place the shiny side towards your seedlings.
- ❑ When planting seeds or seedlings ALWAYS put a marker with them with the name and date.

- Use a disposable syringe to water young seedlings. The seedlings aren't knocked over by the force of the water.
- You can take cuttings of most favourite annuals to keep through the winter. Some annuals that grow well from cuttings are lantana, scaveola, ibosa, impatiens, and some types of begonia to name a few. Pinch off any flowers, and dip the bottom of the stalks in root hormone powder to give the plants more energy into producing roots.
- When starting new plants from cuttings, put a little sugar in the water. It helps the cuttings to root a little faster!
- Instant compost is a great booster for perennials in summer. Accumulate kitchen scraps, no meat or fat, put in a blender, and add water and 1 teaspoonful of Epsom salts. Spread a half-cup or so around the base of your plant and gently work it into the soil.
- Don't add gravel to your pots when planting as this constricts the root system; use a potting mix that has vermiculite in it to keep the soil loose.
- When replanting seedlings that have sprouted, mix a crushed vitamin $B_{12}$ tablet with the water in the watering-can, and pour it into the hole before the seedlings go in. This will give the seedlings a boost of vitamins to get them off to a good start.
- To get rid of weeds in a flower-bed you want to dig over, cover the ground in several layers of black plastic bags and leave until the weeds rot or die.
- To avoid over-watering house-plants, water from the top and stop watering when the liquid appears at the bottom of the plant. Leave to stand in a shallow container for a quarter of an hour before removing the excess water.
- If you are uncertain about whether your plants need watering, take a piece of newspaper and dab it lightly onto the soil. Gently press and remove. If the paper is damp, the plant has enough water.

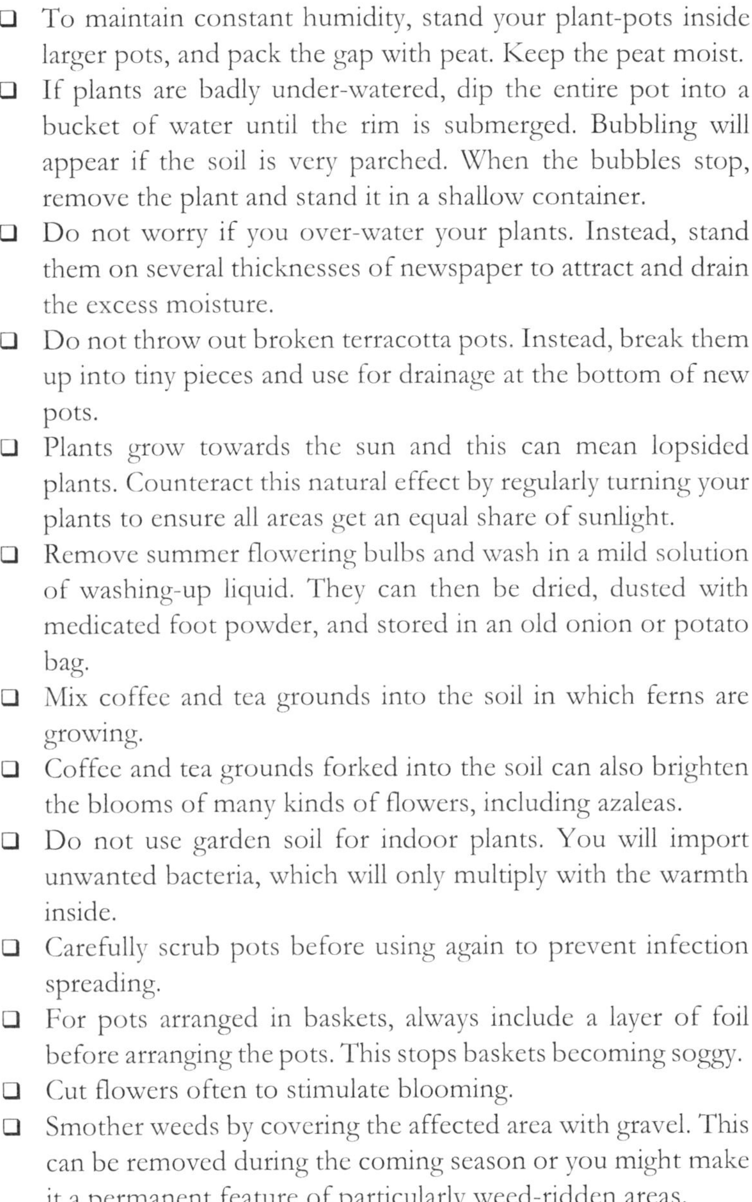

- ❑ To maintain constant humidity, stand your plant-pots inside larger pots, and pack the gap with peat. Keep the peat moist.
- ❑ If plants are badly under-watered, dip the entire pot into a bucket of water until the rim is submerged. Bubbling will appear if the soil is very parched. When the bubbles stop, remove the plant and stand it in a shallow container.
- ❑ Do not worry if you over-water your plants. Instead, stand them on several thicknesses of newspaper to attract and drain the excess moisture.
- ❑ Do not throw out broken terracotta pots. Instead, break them up into tiny pieces and use for drainage at the bottom of new pots.
- ❑ Plants grow towards the sun and this can mean lopsided plants. Counteract this natural effect by regularly turning your plants to ensure all areas get an equal share of sunlight.
- ❑ Remove summer flowering bulbs and wash in a mild solution of washing-up liquid. They can then be dried, dusted with medicated foot powder, and stored in an old onion or potato bag.
- ❑ Mix coffee and tea grounds into the soil in which ferns are growing.
- ❑ Coffee and tea grounds forked into the soil can also brighten the blooms of many kinds of flowers, including azaleas.
- ❑ Do not use garden soil for indoor plants. You will import unwanted bacteria, which will only multiply with the warmth inside.
- ❑ Carefully scrub pots before using again to prevent infection spreading.
- ❑ For pots arranged in baskets, always include a layer of foil before arranging the pots. This stops baskets becoming soggy.
- ❑ Cut flowers often to stimulate blooming.
- ❑ Smother weeds by covering the affected area with gravel. This can be removed during the coming season or you might make it a permanent feature of particularly weed-ridden areas.

- ❑ Store bulbs packed into old tights or stockings before hanging them up to let the air circulate around them.
- ❑ Moisten bulb fibre by punching holes in the bag it comes in. Immerse the bag in a bucket of water until the fibre is well soaked. Squeeze out as much excess water as you can before using.
- ❑ Tall perennials such as boltonia, autumn aster, and chrysanthemum need staking before they start falling over. At this stage, it's too late to place the round grow-through-type supports over plants. Instead, use the linking stakes that surround plants, using as many stakes as you need.
- ❑ Madonna lily bulbs should be planted 5 to 7cm deep. Older bulbs may be dug up and divided. Incorporate some sand into the soil under and around them to improve soil drainage and prevent rotting.
- ❑ To keep annual flowers such as calendulas and petunias looking their best, deadhead the old flowers and continue to water them deeply at least once a week. Feed the plants with a water-soluble fertiliser to promote more foliage growth and assure a good supply of blooms until frost.
- ❑ Help outdoor plants adjust to being stored indoors during the winter months by leaving them outside during the day, and bringing them indoors at night.

## HOME RECIPES FOR FLOWER-BED TREATMENTS

### Soil Conditioning Tonic

This tonic is especially useful in spring, when soil really needs a tonic to recover from the ravages of winter.

*Ingredients:*

10kg garden food
5kg gypsum
1kg diatomaceous earth
450g sugar

*Method:*
Mix the ingredients and distribute through a hand-held broadcast spreader on a medium setting. Dig deeply into the soil.
Apply a thin layer of fresh grass cuttings on top and fork well in.

**Spring Spray**
*Ingredients:*
1 can of beer
1 tbsp washing-up liquid
1 tbsp antiseptic mouthwash
$^1/_4$ tsp instant tea granules
*Method:*
Combine ingredients in a 5-litre hose sprayer and fill the balance of the jar with regular cola. Use to over-spray flowers.

**Special Treat for Bulbs, Tubers and Corms**
Treat bulbs, tubers and corms just before planting by soaking them in a solution of:
1 can of beer
2 tbsp washing-up liquid
$^1/_4$ tsp instant tea granules
2 gallons tepid water

**Spring Tonic**
*Ingredients:*
25g liquid lawn food
Vitamin $B_1$ plant food starter
2 cups of bone-meal
6 tbsp sugar

*Method:*
Mix bone-meal and the sugar and add to the soil used for planting flowers, small fruit or vegetables in containers. Then dampen the soil and add the remaining ingredients mixed with 4 litres of water.

**Spring Bath for Perennials and Above-the-Ground Bulbs**
Just after planting, bathe in the following tonic:
*Ingredients:*
1 tbsp washing-up liquid
1 tbsp chewing tobacco juice
1 tbsp antiseptic mouthwash
1 drop of Tabasco sauce
*Method:*
Combine ingredients in a 5-litre hose sprayer, filling the rest of the jar with water.

**Super Flower Tonic**
Just after planting, feed flowers every morning with the following tonic.
*Ingredients:*
1 can of beer
1 tbsp ammonia
1 tbsp washing-up liquid
1 tbsp liquid lawn food
1 tbsp molasses
1 drop of Tabasco sauce
*Method:*
Combine ingredients in a 5-litre hose sprayer, topped up with warm water.

**Summer Tonic for Flowers**
This tonic is excellent for discouraging insects and disease.
*Ingredients:*
1 tbsp washing-up liquid

1 tbsp chewing tobacco juice
1 tbsp antiseptic mouthwash
*Method:*
Combine ingredients in a 5-litre hose sprayer, topped up with warm water.

Any of the soil fumigants applied to flower-beds during autumn will kill off wireworm and various other harmful creatures. To make your own fumigant, use crude naphthalene.

**Summer Booster**
*Ingredients:*
1 tbsp fertiliser for outdoor plants
½ tsp gelatine
½ tsp washing-up liquid
½ tsp corn syrup
¼ tsp tea granules
1 capful of whiskey
*Method:*
Mix ingredients with 1 gallon of water and store in an airtight container. Add ½ cup of the solution to every 5 litres of water needed to water plants.

**Autumn Tonic for Outdoor and Indoor Plants**
*Ingredients:*
1 tbsp washing-up liquid
Dursban at recommended rate
*Method:*
Combine ingredients into a 5-litre hose sprayer, topped up with warm water. Use to wash plants thoroughly before storing during the winter months.

**Autumn Booster**

This tonic is for bulbs planted in the autumn.

*Ingredients:*

5kg dehydrated manure or compost
2.5kg bone-meal
450g Epsom salts

*Method:*

Combine ingredients and add up to 7kg of fireplace ashes. Dig into the soil around the bulbs.

**Autumn Over-spray**

*Ingredients:*

1 can of beer
1 can of regular cola
1 tbsp washing-up liquid
1 tbsp chewing tobacco juice

*Method:*

Mix ingredients and over-spray flowers using a hand-held sprayer. Cover flower-beds with recent grass cuttings to which is added:

1 can of regular cola
1 tbsp washing-up liquid
1 tbsp ammonia

*Method:*

Mix ingredients and add to a 5-litre hose sprayer, topping up the jar with tepid water. Fork gently into flower-beds.

## Section 3

# Water Gardens

More and more people have discovered that the movement of water can bring their garden to life. No other part of the garden displays such transient seasonal changes, as well as adding another dimension to your garden.

If you are going to create an ecological home for pond life the pond will need at least four to six hours of sunlight a day. You must also select a site that is close to the house, where you can obtain access to an electrical source, so that you can see your water feature from indoors.

Your first decision is to decide the shape and size of your pond. Remember that if you want fish in your pond, the depth should be at least 45cm. The size of the pump for circulation and aeration of the water will depend on the size of the pond. A small pump, from 300 to 600 litres output, will be enough to run a stream of water through a small fountain head. There are many ornamental fountain tops to choose from. Favourites are brass frogs, fish, and heron. There are also fixtures that will spray water in a fan shape, mushroom configuration, or in multiple streams of water. Larger size ponds require a filtration system, which are either mechanical or biological. Mechanical filters are usually submerged in the pond, whereas biological filters are generally sited outside of the pond with the pond water passing through them. Biological filters collect pond pollutants by settling out the solid wastes in a chamber designed to catch large particles.

There are many ways to line your pond. Among the most popular is the preformed rigid fibreglass liner, which is very strong, and is usually used in the small garden. The other type of liner is made from PVC, or flexible rubber, which you have to form into the shape of the hole that you have dug for the pond. The PVC liners are inexpensive, are only 20ml thick, and yet have guarantees of five to ten years. Preformed rigid liners, while simple in appearance, can be quite difficult to install. For the greatest design options, the flexible liners are the best overall.

Once you have decided on the site for your water garden, level the ground, getting rid of stones, rubble, and any large roots from trees and shrubs. When creating a pond using a rigid liner, dig a hole just a bit larger than the volume and shape of the liner. For PVC and rubber liners, draw simple curves with sand to mark out the shape of your pond, and then dig the hole to the required width and depth.

A waterfall creates an interesting feature in any water garden, regardless of size. You can easily make your own waterfall to add movement to the water, by adding height to the ground at one end of your pond with the soil that you have removed when digging the hole.

Line the hole with soft sand to a depth of about 5cm. This is to prevent any sharp stones in the soil from penetrating the lining. PVC and rubber liners should be draped loosely into the hole and smoothed. Anchor the edges with smooth rocks. Fill with water, then smooth again as the liner settles.

Bury any excess liner, but don't cut. With additional rocks, completely line the perimeter of the pond. Assemble the filter box, valve, and fountain head to the pump. You can place the pump in the bottom of the pond. Pumps are very cheap to use, and you should always keep the pump on – even during the night.

Put a thin layer of rocks on the bottom of the pond. Water-plants can be put into baskets, which you can fill with special soil for water-plants.

## TIPS

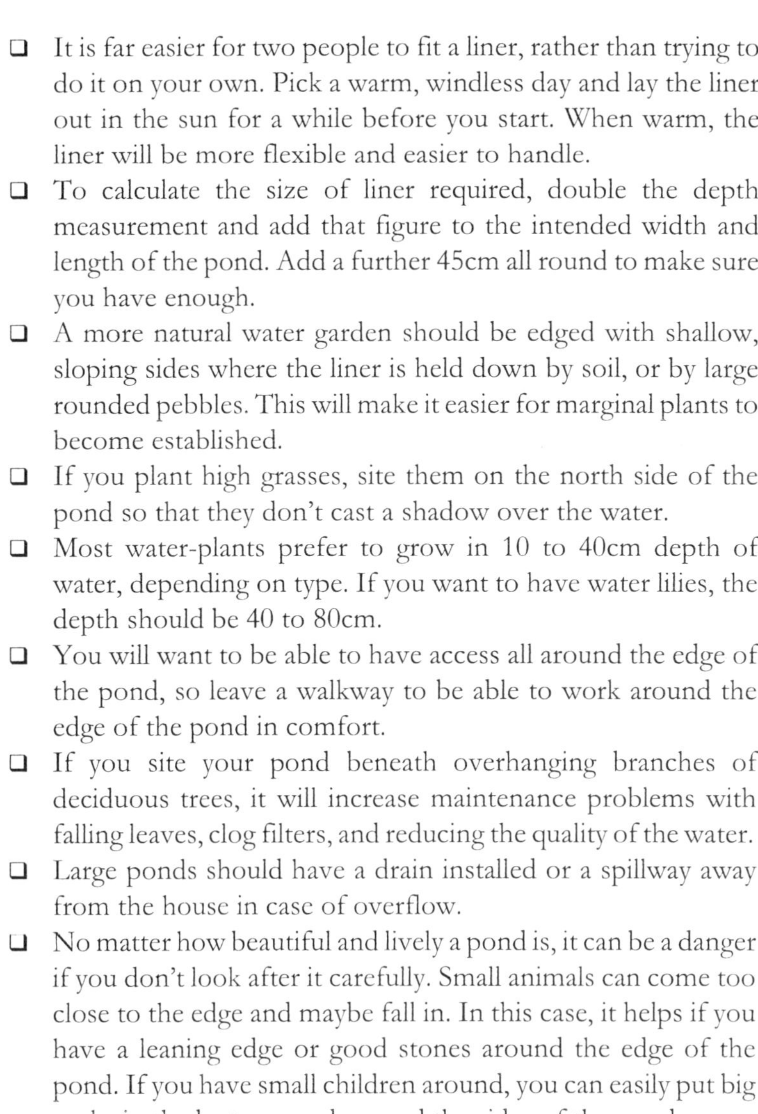

- ❑ It is far easier for two people to fit a liner, rather than trying to do it on your own. Pick a warm, windless day and lay the liner out in the sun for a while before you start. When warm, the liner will be more flexible and easier to handle.
- ❑ To calculate the size of liner required, double the depth measurement and add that figure to the intended width and length of the pond. Add a further 45cm all round to make sure you have enough.
- ❑ A more natural water garden should be edged with shallow, sloping sides where the liner is held down by soil, or by large rounded pebbles. This will make it easier for marginal plants to become established.
- ❑ If you plant high grasses, site them on the north side of the pond so that they don't cast a shadow over the water.
- ❑ Most water-plants prefer to grow in 10 to 40cm depth of water, depending on type. If you want to have water lilies, the depth should be 40 to 80cm.
- ❑ You will want to be able to have access all around the edge of the pond, so leave a walkway to be able to work around the edge of the pond in comfort.
- ❑ If you site your pond beneath overhanging branches of deciduous trees, it will increase maintenance problems with falling leaves, clog filters, and reducing the quality of the water.
- ❑ Large ponds should have a drain installed or a spillway away from the house in case of overflow.
- ❑ No matter how beautiful and lively a pond is, it can be a danger if you don't look after it carefully. Small animals can come too close to the edge and maybe fall in. In this case, it helps if you have a leaning edge or good stones around the edge of the pond. If you have small children around, you can easily put big rocks in the bottom, and around the sides of the pond.

- New ponds can have 2.5cm of fish per 75 square cm of pond surface. Older, established ponds could sustain 5 to 7.5cm of fish per 75 square cm of pond surface.
- You should not feed your fish more than they can consume in five minutes. Give your fish a high protein feed in the summer, to help them build up a healthy fat layer to survive the winter. In the spring and autumn, it is best to feed them wheat germ or other low-protein food because it is easily digested.
- Oxygenating plants are vital in a water garden. They absorb impurities from the water, which helps to prevent algae growth. To oxygenate your pond, plant one bunch of oxygenating plants for every 150 square cm of pond surface. Pot the plants in washed pea gravel; several bunches can be placed in the same pot. The pots should be anchored and placed on the bottom of the pond. These plants thrive on the same nutrients that algae use to grow. Sufficient plants will greatly reduce algae in your pond. They absorb the carbon dioxide that fish produce, and liberate oxygen for the fish to live. Fish spawn and lay eggs in oxygenating plants. Baby fish use these plants for shelter.
- Potted surface plants such as lilies need at least five hours of sun per day to flower and should be fertilised on a regular basis. Remember lilies do not like water splashed on them. Place them away from waterfalls and fountains.
- Pumps must run 24 hours a day. Good bacteria (aerobic bacteria) can die if the pump is stopped for even four hours.
- Where turf is grown up to the edge of the pond, consider allowing a narrow band of the waterside grasses to grow tall, to create a more natural effect. Marginal plants can then be encouraged to merge with that part of the lawn.
- Marginal, or bog plants are aquatic plants, which grow in shallow water and are commonly found along the water's edge. There are many varieties of marginal plants that will add height and texture to the water garden. Some stand above the

water while others rest on the water's surface. Some marginals add a handsome display of foliage while others will create constant blooms throughout the season. Lush, green foliage, with accents of pink, white, and yellow can be obtained. Plants must be fed regularly.

- Floating plants are desirable and fascinating as they add colour and shade to a pond. They do not require planting, although some varieties perform better if planted first. Others, you can simply float in the pond. Due to the shade given by floating plants, they are ideal for ponds with an algae problem. Roots provide fish spawning beds and protection for new-borns. All floating plants should be removed from the pond before frost.
- Once winter approaches and the water temperature of the pond drops, the hardy lilies automatically go dormant. If any new leaves appear, they will be very small and will remain under the water, close to the soil. As the old foliage browns, simply prune and lower the lily to the deepest part of the pond. If a sufficient depth of water can be maintained so that freezing does not occur at the root level, the hardy lily does not need to be removed from the pond.
- Use a mesh net cover over your pond to keep leaves, twigs and other debris out of the water. If a net is not used it is important to remove leaves as some leaves can turn the water brown and can be toxic to fish.
- When preparing your water garden for the winter, cut plants to 15cm from the top of the pot and place on the bottom of the pond after the first heavy frost. However, hollow stemmed plants should be trimmed above the water line. Trimming these below the water line could cause rotting.
- Oxygenating plants should be cut back to 5 to 7.5cm above their containers, and placed on the bottom of the pond. Decaying plants will foul water quality and should be removed from the pond.

SECTION 4

# Building Your Own Rock Garden

When selecting the best site for your rock garden, take into account the size of your garden, and choose a site that will most effectively enhance your property, as well as your enjoyment of your garden. Most often, experts advise gardeners with older properties to locate the rock garden well out of sight of buildings and other formal features. However, many modern homes have small gardens limiting the space to the immediate vicinity of the house; so nowadays it's considered quite proper to site a rock garden adjacent to a building, or have it as a centrepiece for a lawn. Areas in gardens where you have a slope, or steep bank, whether natural or created, make an ideal site to place your rock garden.

The secret of building a successful rock garden lies in making the whole structure of the garden look natural. To do this, rocks must be placed to give the effect that they were positioned by nature without help from the gardener. To obtain a natural effect, use the same type of rock throughout the garden, or at least throughout major parts of it. Position each piece of rock so that it appears that it's an enormous rock with only the tips of its peaks showing above the surface and except for narrow clefts, it should appear to be connected with neighbouring pieces underground. Rocks that contain stratification lines give a very pleasing look to the eye; these should lay with the strata lines all in one direction, to give a more convincingly natural look.

When laying out a new rock garden your first task is to make a careful survey of the site. Then clear the area of unwanted vegetation by digging out all roots completely. Prune any shrubs or trees that you wish to retain in the area so that they don't overwhelm the rockery. If you have a well located deep-rooted tree in the area, it can be included in the scheme of your layout, to provide some light shade for part of each day in summer.

Once you have decided on the contour of your rock garden, it will be necessary to work the soil to a depth of at least 30cm. You may even have to replace the topsoil. If the soil is not sufficiently porous, mix in generous amounts of coarse sand, grit, or small chips of stone, and if woodland plants are to be grown add a mixture of leaf mould, peat moss, or other suitable partially decayed organic material. If a section of the garden is to be devoted to plants that need alkaline soil, crushed limestone or limestone chips may be included in the topsoil mix.

When positioning the rocks begin at the lowest levels and work upward, setting each piece with its most attractive weathered side exposed, and with its top sloped slightly backward to direct rain or water from sprinklers to the roots. Ensure that each rock is established firmly in its place, and shows off its best aspects. It may be advisable sometimes to prop larger rocks on several smaller ones, and then fill the spaces in between with firmly packed soil.

Make certain there is an adequate depth of soil, especially in the crevices and crannies you intend to plant. It is usually desirable to rake out existing soil and, if necessary after deepening or enlarging the clefts or crevices, to replace it with a better mix, firmly packed, so no voids are left.

Planting is best done in early autumn or early spring. Whenever practicable it is best to delay planting to allow the soil to settle, and to permit clearing the soil of weeds to ensure clean planting areas. Be sure to pull up every weed as soon as it shows above ground.

Choose a selection of plants suitable for natural rock gardens, and if possible, natural to the area in which you live. Your selection should include a variety of shapes, such as spires, globes, and ground cover, and aim for a succession of colour from foliage and flowers throughout the year.

To look natural in their new environment, position your plants in the same way they would grow on natural rocky sites. Seek inspiration from such places, noting the unrestrained informality that prevails.

## TIPS

- ❑ Choose rocks that are porous, rather than hard impervious types such as granite, or hard sandstone.
- ❑ Limestone, particularly water-worn limestone, is one of the most beautiful rocks, but should not be used when planting acid soil plants such as heathers, and rhododendrons.
- ❑ Tufa, a soft lightweight, porous limestone-type rock formed by calcium carbonate deposited in springs and streams, is easy to handle and congenial to plants, but of undistinguished appearance.
- ❑ Hard rocks can be used, but take longer to weather because they are less encouraging to the growth of mosses, lichens and other primitive vegetation that soon conceal freshly exposed portions of softer rocks.
- ❑ Unless no other is available do not use newly-quarried rock. Its raw surfaces are likely to take a long time to weather and, even worse, may display marks of drilling.
- ❑ Weathered pieces collected from the surface of the ground and of a character and colour that suggest age, are likely to be ideal.
- ❑ In some parts of the country suitable material can be obtained from old stone walls. The pieces must be of manageable sizes and of acceptable relation to the size of the garden.
- ❑ By careful placement, it is possible to arrange several comparatively small rocks so that they appear to be a flawed

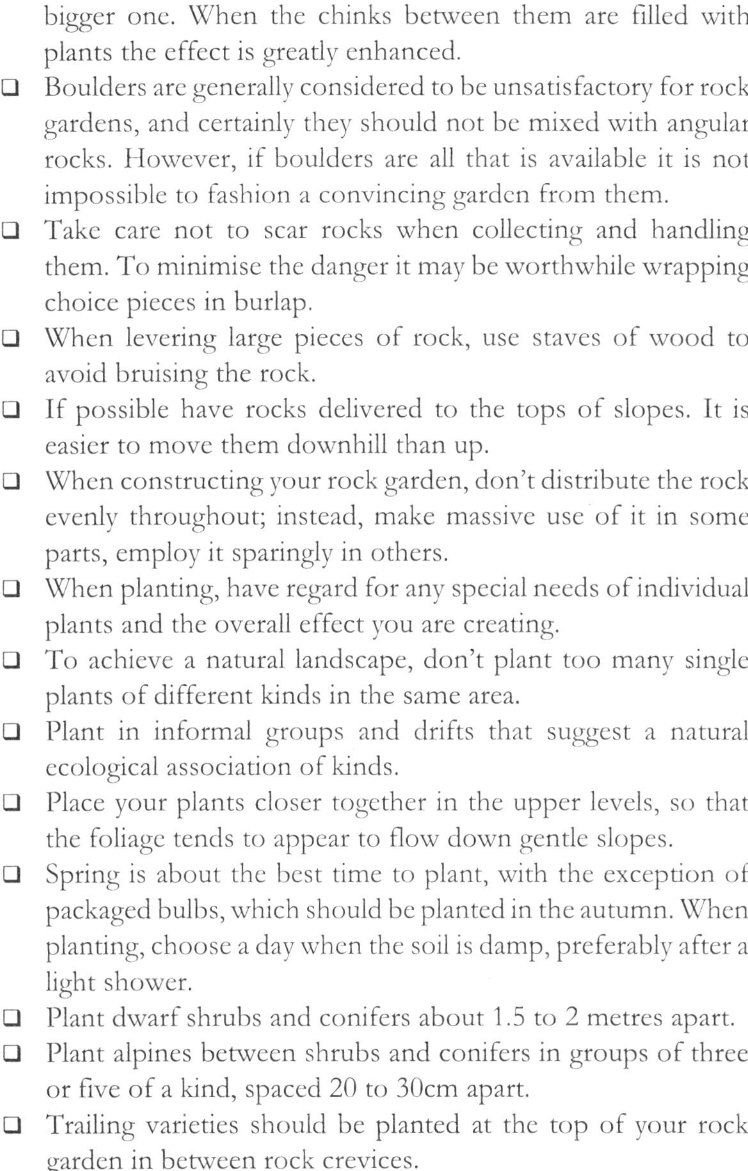

bigger one. When the chinks between them are filled with plants the effect is greatly enhanced.

- ❑ Boulders are generally considered to be unsatisfactory for rock gardens, and certainly they should not be mixed with angular rocks. However, if boulders are all that is available it is not impossible to fashion a convincing garden from them.
- ❑ Take care not to scar rocks when collecting and handling them. To minimise the danger it may be worthwhile wrapping choice pieces in burlap.
- ❑ When levering large pieces of rock, use staves of wood to avoid bruising the rock.
- ❑ If possible have rocks delivered to the tops of slopes. It is easier to move them downhill than up.
- ❑ When constructing your rock garden, don't distribute the rock evenly throughout; instead, make massive use of it in some parts, employ it sparingly in others.
- ❑ When planting, have regard for any special needs of individual plants and the overall effect you are creating.
- ❑ To achieve a natural landscape, don't plant too many single plants of different kinds in the same area.
- ❑ Plant in informal groups and drifts that suggest a natural ecological association of kinds.
- ❑ Place your plants closer together in the upper levels, so that the foliage tends to appear to flow down gentle slopes.
- ❑ Spring is about the best time to plant, with the exception of packaged bulbs, which should be planted in the autumn. When planting, choose a day when the soil is damp, preferably after a light shower.
- ❑ Plant dwarf shrubs and conifers about 1.5 to 2 metres apart.
- ❑ Plant alpines between shrubs and conifers in groups of three or five of a kind, spaced 20 to 30cm apart.
- ❑ Trailing varieties should be planted at the top of your rock garden in between rock crevices.

- ❑ When buying and storing plants in advance of planting, make sure the roots are protected from exposure to sun and wind.
- ❑ Space individual plants with relation to the amount of top growth they are expected to make.
- ❑ Don't break the balls of soil in which roots are growing, but spread roots not encased in soil in their natural positions and work soil between them.
- ❑ Set new plants at the same depth or very slightly deeper than they were previously, firm the soil around them, and soak with a fine spray of water.
- ❑ The surface between individual plants should be mulched lightly with chippings. For the best effect, see that the stone chips consist of a mixture of sizes and are of the same or closely matching kind of rock to that of which the rock garden is constructed.
- ❑ Woodland plants in shaded areas should be mulched with leaf mould, or peat moss, mixed with grit or coarse sand.
- ❑ Most rock garden plants flourish in poor soil conditions, and become too lush and overgrown in those that are too fertile.
- ❑ Scree beds are very simple to add to your rock garden, as well as for growing alpines. Excavate a bed to approximately 1 metre deep on a slope. Place draining material approximately 20 to 30cm deep, then finish with the scree material such as two parts rock chippings, one part compost, and one part good loam.
- ❑ When adding fertiliser, prevent it from being washed to the lower reaches of your rockery when it rains, by stirring it into the top few centimetres of the soil with a hand fork. In this way, the nutrients will filter down to the roots of the plants that you intended to feed.

**Dwarf conifers to choose are:**

Chamaecyparis Obtusa Nana Gracilis
Picea Gregoryana
Picea Mariana Nana

Chamaecyparis Lawsoniana Minima Aurea
Chamaecyparis Lawsoniana Ellwood's Gold
Juniperus Communis Compressa
Thuja Orientalis Aurea Nana
**Dwarf Bulbs** should be grown in groups of one variety together to create a real show:
Crocus
Iris
Narcissus
Puschkinia
Tulip
**Dwarf Shrubs** to choose are:
Rhododendrons
Haberleas
Ramondas
Gaultherias
Vacciniums
Genista Lidia
Hebe Red Edge
Hebe Pinquifolia Pagei
Miniature Roses
Spiraca Little Princess
**Alpines** – remember that most alpines are lime-loving plants:
Alyssum
Arabis
Armeria
Campanula
Dianthus
Helianthemum
Iberis
Phlox
Saxifrages
Thymes

## Section 5

# Roses In The Garden

Nowadays roses are available for sale in container pots enabling you to plant at any time of the year, except of course, when the soil is cold and frosty. With such a variety of species from which to choose, selecting the right type of rose can be a bewildering task. I have therefore, set out a few basic guidelines to help.

### PREPARATION

Roses should be planted in a sunny position away from cold winds, and be given plenty of space between plants to allow the air to circulate. The soil should be fertile and well-drained.

When you have selected the site for planting, carefully dig the soil to a depth of one spit, that is, the depth of your spade blade or the tines of your fork, and ensure that the site is weed-free.

Add a good-quality rose fertiliser to the whole area, and dig-in composted bark to improve the soil structure. On no account use fresh manure when planting.

### PLANTING

Dig a hole large enough to accommodate the roots. Add peat moss or compost and mix well with the soil. Place some of the mixture at the bottom of the hole.

Position the rose in the hole so that the bud union is at or just above ground level. In cooler climates, position the bud union a few centimetres below ground level and mulch over. Work the soil mixture around the roots to eliminate any air pockets, then firm the soil around the roots and add more soil until the hole is full.

Water the surface soil, and let it soak in, then spread a layer of composted bark around the plant to protect it from drying out. Trim canes back to 20cm, making 45-degree angle cuts just above outward facing buds.

To prevent newly-planted roses from drying out, water daily for two or three weeks after planting. Roses like a rich, fertile soil and will respond well to regular feeding during the spring and summer.

**Bush Roses**

The Floribunda bears a great number of small flowers, making them very popular with rose growing enthusiasts. They are particularly striking when planted in groups, but are just as impressive planted singly.

Hybrid Tea roses bear medium- or large-sized shapely blooms with petals forming a distinctive central cone.

Both Floribunda and Hybrid Teas will grow to a height of 75 to 150cm. They should be planted 60 to 90cm apart.

Prune during March, old stems can be hard pruned to encourage new growth, and last year's growth lightly pruned to give a longer flowering period.

**Miniature Roses**

Because the leaves and flowers are small, these roses are increasingly popular due to their novelty and versatile nature. They are ideal for rockeries, edging beds, and pots. They will grow to a height of 30 to 45cm. Plant 30cm apart.

Do not prune when newly-planted. Once established, simply remove dead or poor wood and trim to shape with a pair of secateurs in March each year.

### Patio Roses

These are a fairly new species that have been grown for their compact size. They can be planted into pots or tubs where their colourful blooms will add interest beside a door, or on the patio. They also make good subjects in borders or beds of the own, especially to the front of a house in a small garden. They will grow to a height of 30 to 60cm. Plant 60 to 75cm apart.

As with all potted plants, patio roses need plenty of light and water.

### Climbers and Ramblers

Climbers have large blooms and stiff stems, whereas ramblers have groups of small flowers and long, pliable stems.

Climbers and ramblers are ideal for covering walls, screens, fences, trellis arches, and pergolas. A strong growing climber or rambler rose will cover a space of wall at least 4 metres in length.

Tie in the branches as they develop. For an arch or porchway one rambler rose on either side is ample, but it is not wise to mingle varieties in such a position.

With an extended line of arches or a pergola, roses may be planted in pairs at intervals of not less than 3 metres.

Climbers and ramblers should not be pruned until spring. Pruning may be done immediately before planting where there is danger of rough winds catching the growths, and thus loosening the plants in the soil, but the cutting must not be so severe as the real spring pruning.

Rambler roses may have two or three of the strongest growths left uncut for the first year, to flower right away, but it is best to cut back the remainder of the growths to within 15cm of the ground. After the first year, pruning ramblers consists of cutting away wood that has flowered, doing this as soon as possible after flowering is finished. Tie into place the best shoots made during the preceding summer.

### Shrub Roses

These are ideal for growing in borders. Some varieties can also be used for hedging. They will grow to a height of 100 to 200cm. Plant 90 to 120cm apart.

Shrub roses need little pruning. Simply cut out a proportion of the older wood, right down to the base each winter to encourage new shoots.

### Standard Roses

This is a bush rose that has been trained on a tall stem and can be used to give height to borders, giving flowers at eye level. Plant 150cm apart.

When pruning standard roses, remove all dead wood, cutting it away right from the base. Remove all the weak, thin wood, which climbs up the centre of the bush. Shorten the outside branches at your own discretion to give the bush a good shape.

## TIPS

- ❑ When buying roses in pots, make sure that the soil in the pot is not dried out. If it is, don't buy it! You can tell if it is dry because the pot will feel light when you pick it up.
- ❑ The roots of roses bought by mail order will need water. Soak the roots in a bucket of water for a few hours before planting.
- ❑ The importance of watering cannot be stressed enough. Proper watering is vital to restore moisture lost to high temperatures and wind. It is best to water infrequently, but deeply. Plants in sunny locations can be watered twice a day in hot weather, especially when it's windy. Watering in the early morning and late evening is best. Keep in mind, however, that giving roses in containers extra watering will deplete the plants of fertiliser by washing it out of the soil.

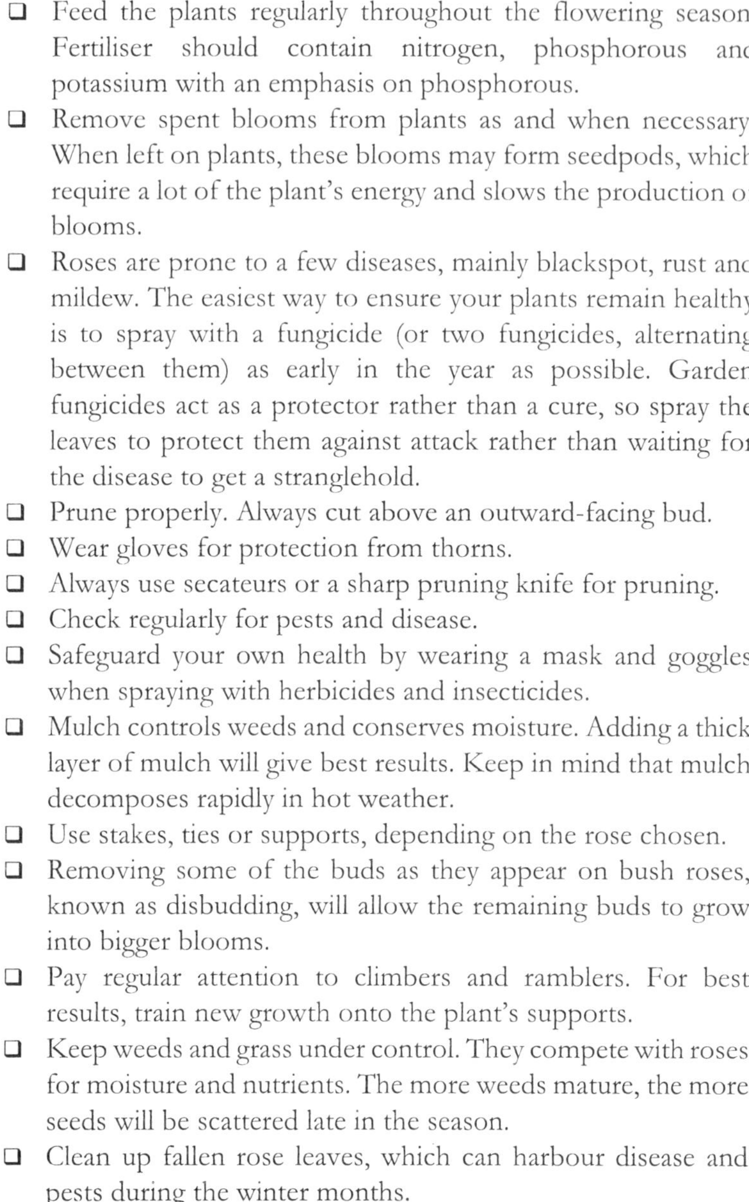

- Feed the plants regularly throughout the flowering season. Fertiliser should contain nitrogen, phosphorous and potassium with an emphasis on phosphorous.
- Remove spent blooms from plants as and when necessary. When left on plants, these blooms may form seedpods, which require a lot of the plant's energy and slows the production of blooms.
- Roses are prone to a few diseases, mainly blackspot, rust and mildew. The easiest way to ensure your plants remain healthy is to spray with a fungicide (or two fungicides, alternating between them) as early in the year as possible. Garden fungicides act as a protector rather than a cure, so spray the leaves to protect them against attack rather than waiting for the disease to get a stranglehold.
- Prune properly. Always cut above an outward-facing bud.
- Wear gloves for protection from thorns.
- Always use secateurs or a sharp pruning knife for pruning.
- Check regularly for pests and disease.
- Safeguard your own health by wearing a mask and goggles when spraying with herbicides and insecticides.
- Mulch controls weeds and conserves moisture. Adding a thick layer of mulch will give best results. Keep in mind that mulch decomposes rapidly in hot weather.
- Use stakes, ties or supports, depending on the rose chosen.
- Removing some of the buds as they appear on bush roses, known as disbudding, will allow the remaining buds to grow into bigger blooms.
- Pay regular attention to climbers and ramblers. For best results, train new growth onto the plant's supports.
- Keep weeds and grass under control. They compete with roses for moisture and nutrients. The more weeds mature, the more seeds will be scattered late in the season.
- Clean up fallen rose leaves, which can harbour disease and pests during the winter months.

- ❑ Plant chives under rose bushes to help control aphids.
- ❑ Put willow branches in a large pail, then cover them with water, and let them sit for two weeks. Use the liquid as a fertiliser to water your roses.
- ❑ To protect your hands from sharp thorns on rose bushes, hold the rose with a clothes-peg when cutting them for bouquets or when pruning.
- ❑ Cut roses regularly, to encourage new flower growth. Cut the stems slightly above five-leaf clusters. Seal the cuts with nail polish and dust with powdered soil.

## HOME RECIPES FOR ROSE TREATMENTS

### Spring Tonic for Roses

This is a highly effective tonic for bare-root rose bushes you've recently acquired. Dip the whole bush, roots and all, into a bucket of warm water to which the following tonic has been added:
1 tbsp washing-up liquid
¼ tsp liquid bleach

Just before planting, soak rose bushes for 30 minutes in a clean bucket of warm water to which is added a mixture of:
1 tsp washing-up liquid
1 tsp ammonia
2 tbsp corn syrup

When planting rose bushes, sprinkle the following mixture in the soil:
75% bone-meal
25% Epsom salts
½ tsp sugar for each 4 handfuls of the bone-meal/Epsom salts mixture

After planting, add 2 cupfuls of the following mixture to each rose bed:
1 tsp washing-up liquid
1 tsp Vitamin $B_1$

1 tsp Hydrogen Peroxide
1 capful whiskey
2.5 litres of warm tea water

**Super Tonic for Pre-spring Pruning**

*Ingredients:*
1 cup of washing-up liquid
1 cup of chewing tobacco juice
1 cup of antiseptic mouthwash

*Method:*
Add mixture to a 100-litre water barrel, topping up with warm water. Use a sprayer to bathe roses every fortnight for the remainder of the growing season using the same mixture, which can be stored until needed.

**Spring Tonic for Established Roses**

*Ingredients:*
2.5kg garden compost
1 cup of Epsom salts
1 cup of sugar
4 dried, crushed banana skins
2 cups of bone-meal

*Method:*
Combine ingredients and apply to surface of rose beds.

**Summer Tonic for Established Roses**

*Ingredients:*
1 can of beer
1 cup of ammonia
½ cup of washing-up liquid
½ cup of liquid lawn food
½ cup of molasses

*Method:*
Add to a 100-litre water barrel and top up with warm water. Feed to

rose bushes once every three weeks, in the morning, for the entire growing season.

**Aphid Spray for Roses**

*Ingredients:*

Makes 3 litres

450g elder or rhubarb leaves, or

200g wormwood leaves

3 litres of water

*Method:*

Chop the leaves and place in a large saucepan with one third of the water. Boil and reduce to simmer for half an hour. Strain and reject the leaves. Add the remaining water to the liquid and leave to cool. Place in a spray bottle and use against aphids on roses and other affected plants.

**Aphid Control Spray**

*Ingredients:*

1 cup of chopped onions or shallots

1 cup of water

*Method:*

Purée onions or shallots in a blender or food processor until fine. Add water and use in hand-held sprayer.

SECTION 6

# Garden Trees

Trees create a focal point, as well as giving shade, privacy, and a sense of permanence. Most of all, they are a haven for birds, bringing life and movement into your garden. Whether you want colourful leaves or bark, or fruit trees to supply you with luscious fruit in the autumn and blossom in the spring, there is a tree to satisfy the needs of everyone.

Before buying your tree, it's important to remember that large growing varieties may cause damage to the foundations of buildings and paths nearby, so it would be wise to plant large trees at least 30 metres distant to prevent such damage. Also, try to avoid planting trees where they will shade light from windows, or overhang neighbours' gardens.

## PLANTING

Your first task when planting is to select a site that is in full sun. Clear the area of any weeds and rubble, and then dig a hole twice as wide as the root ball, and no deeper than the height of the root ball. The soil that you dig out of the hole can be used to backfill around the root ball. Fork the soil in the bottom of the hole, and mix in garden compost or planting compost, and a general fertiliser such as bone-meal.

Gently tap the tree out of its container and tease out any congested roots. Place it in the hole, ensuring that the tops of the roots are below soil level. For most trees, staking is required.

Hammer a stake firmly into the hole adjacent to the root ball. The stake should be long enough to give the trunk support up to about half its length to the first lateral branches. Fill in the surrounding hole and firm down the soil, making sure there are no air pockets around the roots. Finally, fit an adjustable tie around both the stake and the trunk. To prevent damage to the trunk, use strong, wide strips of rubber or plastic to support the tree; other options may chaff the bark and introduce infections.

## TIPS

- ❑ Choosing a tree should be a well-thought-out decision, as tree planting can be a significant investment in time and money. Proper selection can provide you with years of enjoyment as well as increasing the value of your property.
- ❑ Newly-planted trees require special care during the first year. The most important requirement is an adequate supply of water. During the spring and summer, trees need to be watered about every seven to ten days throughout the first growing season. Water trees slowly, but deeply. Large trees take longer to establish and it's therefore necessary to water them for two or three years.
- ❑ Generally, it isn't necessary to apply fertiliser to newly-planted trees. Most soils can supply sufficient amounts of nutrients whilst the roots are being established.
- ❑ Applications of fertiliser should be applied to trees for two to three years after planting if they are growing poorly or possess light green foliage. Sprinkle a handful of bone-meal or a general fertiliser around the tree in early spring and again a month later.
- ❑ Trees bought in containers can be planted at any time of the year, but not when the ground is frozen.
- ❑ Deciduous trees will lose their foliage in the autumn until the early spring, so when buying, check them out at the garden

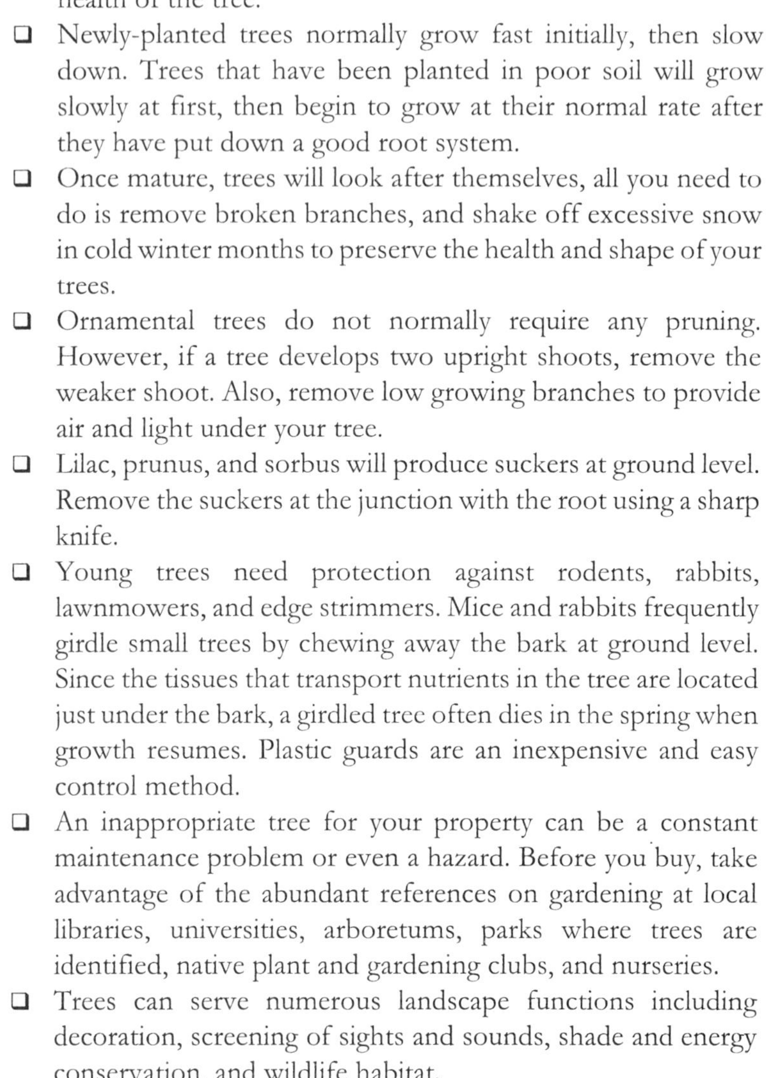

centre early in the summer to give you a conception of the health of the tree.

- ❑ Newly-planted trees normally grow fast initially, then slow down. Trees that have been planted in poor soil will grow slowly at first, then begin to grow at their normal rate after they have put down a good root system.
- ❑ Once mature, trees will look after themselves, all you need to do is remove broken branches, and shake off excessive snow in cold winter months to preserve the health and shape of your trees.
- ❑ Ornamental trees do not normally require any pruning. However, if a tree develops two upright shoots, remove the weaker shoot. Also, remove low growing branches to provide air and light under your tree.
- ❑ Lilac, prunus, and sorbus will produce suckers at ground level. Remove the suckers at the junction with the root using a sharp knife.
- ❑ Young trees need protection against rodents, rabbits, lawnmowers, and edge strimmers. Mice and rabbits frequently girdle small trees by chewing away the bark at ground level. Since the tissues that transport nutrients in the tree are located just under the bark, a girdled tree often dies in the spring when growth resumes. Plastic guards are an inexpensive and easy control method.
- ❑ An inappropriate tree for your property can be a constant maintenance problem or even a hazard. Before you buy, take advantage of the abundant references on gardening at local libraries, universities, arboretums, parks where trees are identified, native plant and gardening clubs, and nurseries.
- ❑ Trees can serve numerous landscape functions including decoration, screening of sights and sounds, shade and energy conservation, and wildlife habitat.
- ❑ Reliable nurseries will not sell plant material that is not suitable for your area. However, some mass marketers have trees and

shrubs that are not winter hardy in the area sold. Even if a tree is hardy, it may not flower consistently from year to year at the limits of its useful range due to late spring frosts.

- ❑ If you are buying a tree for its spring blossom and autumn fruits, select trees native to your area. They will be more tolerant of local weather and soil conditions.
- ❑ When planting a small tree, it is often difficult to imagine that in 20 years it could be shading your entire garden, so make sure you know how big it is likely to grow.
- ❑ Some trees can live for hundreds of years. Others are considered 'short-lived' and may live for only 20 or 30 years. Many short-lived trees tend to be smaller ornamental species. Short-lived species should not necessarily be ruled out when considering plantings. They may have other desirable characteristics, such as size, shape, and tolerance of shade or fruit that would be useful in the landscape. These species may also fill a void in a young landscape, and can be removed as other larger, longer-lived species mature.
- ❑ Plant silver maple (*Acer saccharium*) in a sheltered spot. They are known to have weak wood that is susceptible to damage in heavy winds.
- ❑ Evergreen trees will provide cover and shade all year round. They may also be more effective as a barrier for wind and noise. Deciduous trees will give you summer shade but allow the winter sun to shine in. This may be a consideration for where to place the tree in your garden.
- ❑ Bare root trees are usually extremely small plants. Because there is no soil on the roots, they must be planted when they are dormant to avoid drying out. The roots must be kept moist until planted. Frequently, bare root trees are offered by seed and nursery mail-order catalogues. Bare root trees usually are offered in the early spring and should be planted as soon as possible upon arrival. Carefully follow the planting instructions that come with your tree.

- ❑ Under no circumstances should trees be topped. Not only does this practice ruin the natural shape of the tree, but also increases susceptibility to diseases and results in very narrow crotch angles, the angle between the trunk and the side branch. Narrow crotch angles are weaker than wide ones and more susceptible to damage from wind. If a large tree requires major reduction in height or size, contact a professionally-trained arborist. There are other methods to selectively remove large branches without sacrificing the health or beauty of the tree.
- ❑ Never plant a tree closer than 5 metres to your house. When selecting a tree to plant, keep in mind that after several years it may have heavy surface roots that would make it a difficult tree for a small garden. Research your potential tree. They are expensive to remove if improperly selected or planted.
- ❑ Use a 25-litre plastic bucket with a small hole in the bottom to water newly-planted trees. Just fill the bucket full of water and place at the base of your tree, it will take several hours to drain but will water your new trees slowly.
- ❑ Beat your trees in spring with a rolled-up newspaper to stimulate sap flow.

## HOME RECIPES FOR TREE TREATMENTS

### Spring Treatment

As early as possible, wash trees, shrubs and evergreens with this special spring treatment tonic.

*Ingredients:*

1 tbsp washing-up liquid
1 tbsp chewing tobacco juice
1 tbsp antiseptic mouthwash

*Method:*

Combine the ingredients in a 5-litre hose sprayer, topped with warm water.

**Super Feed**

*Ingredients:*

15 litres garden fertiliser

450g sugar

225g Epsom salts

*Method:*

Mix ingredients. Drill holes at the weep line of trees, 20 to 25cm deep, and 45 to 60cm apart, in circles 60cm diameter. Fill the holes using 2 tablespoonfuls of mixture. The same tonic can be dispensed to shrubs and evergreens using a hand-held broadcast spreader on a medium setting.

**Super Feed Tonic** – can be over-sprayed with the following:

*Ingredients:*

1 can of beer

1 cup of liquid lawn food

1 tbsp washing-up liquid

1 tbsp ammonia

*Method:*

Combine ingredients in a 5-litre hose sprayer, using regular cola to top up the jar.

**Pest Exterminator**

*Ingredients:*

Fruit tree spray at half the recommended measure

1 tbsp washing-up liquid

1 tbsp chewing tobacco juice

1 tbsp antiseptic mouthwash

*Method:*

Combine ingredients in a 5-litre hose sprayer, topped with warm water. Use to spray plants in the late evening.

**Summer Greenery Tonic**
*Ingredients:*
1 can of beer
1 tbsp ammonia
1 tbsp washing-up liquid
(Baby shampoo can be substituted for washing-up liquid)
$^{1}/_{2}$ cup liquid lawn food
1 tbsp molasses
*Method:*
Combine ingredients in a 5-litre hose sprayer, and top up with warm water. Use to feed all members of this group, including maple trees.

**Insect and Disease Repellent**
*Ingredients:*
1 tbsp washing-up liquid
1 tbsp chewing tobacco juice
1 tbsp antiseptic mouthwash
*Method:*
Mix ingredients in a 5-litre hose sprayer, and top up with warm water. Use to spray all affected group members.

**Autumn Tonic**
*Ingredients:*
225g Epsom salts
1 cup of Paradichlorobenzene crystals
*Method:*
Combine ingredients and sprinkle around the roots. Do not use during frosty or wintry conditions.

## SECTION 7

# Garden Conifers

To answer the needs of gardeners many species have been developed from the giants of the forests that will fit perfectly into a small modern garden. These ornamental varieties come in many shapes and forms. Although most conifers are evergreen, there are numerous variations in colour, shape and size to enhance any garden. Some have bluish-grey leaves, others have different shades of green, and there are the variegated ones as well as the golden-leafed specimens.

Good stock suitable for town or country gardens can be obtained from most garden centres. However, when buying, take into account that many trees will grow as much as 30cm or more per year, so the ultimate size of the tree has to be taken into account before making your selection. When you have decided on the size of your trees, look for conifers to provide your garden with interest throughout the year, as well as for their ornamental values.

### PLANTING

It is possible to plant conifers all year round, providing you avoid very cold, wet or drought conditions. Even so, the best time to plant is either spring or early autumn, when temperatures are cooler and rainfall is more abundant. Plant on an overcast day when the soil is damp; this will reduce the chances of the tree becoming dehydrated.

When planting larger varieties, prepare a hole 1 metre wide by 45cm deep. For small trees dig a hole twice the width and twice the height of the root ball. If the soil is very compacted or so light and porous that it retains very little moisture, you will need to add organic matter. Use composted bark and fertiliser, such as 'Growmore' at the rates recommended on the packaging.

Pines, spruces and firs can be sheared in spring when the new growth has just emerged and is still soft, but not at any other time of the year. For this reason, they are much more difficult to maintain as hedges. If you don't mind the work, though, you can create a unique hedge using these plants.

## TIPS

- ❑ When planting a conifer sold in a container, first loosen the roots by firmly tapping around the pot with the palm of your hand. Then, trim any roots that may be growing out of the drainage holes. If the plants are small, place your hand on the top of the pot, spreading your fingers so that the stem and the top of the soil are supported, and carefully slide the plant out, keeping the root ball intact. Tip large containers onto their sides to facilitate this process.
- ❑ Many container-grown plants will have a mass of circling roots that should be carefully loosened by hand or with a small hand fork before planting. This will prevent the roots from girdling and eventually killing the plant.
- ❑ It takes about three to six months for the roots to grow out into the surrounding soil, so for the first month or so, check the plant every two to three days for signs of stress, and water whenever the soil feels dry.
- ❑ Rather than placing conifers at the side or back of your garden, or placing them right in the middle of the lawn, treat them as prime garden plants.
- ❑ Because conifers retain their needles all year-round, they are perfect for framing views and forming backdrops for spring-blooming trees and shrubs.

- You can use a low-growing conifer like a creeping juniper to define space next to a lawn.
- Placed strategically, conifers can be used to screen unsightly views, establish privacy, buffer loud noise, and effectively block strong wind.
- When choosing conifers to combine with flowers, remember to consider colour. Blue conifers look great with pink- and purple-flowering plants, yellow conifers set off yellow flowers, and green conifers complement light-coloured plants and flowers.
- Enthusiastic gardeners who have a large enough garden can select unusual conifers such as a monkey-puzzle tree. Be sure to limit your choice to just one or two types, and don't overdo it with too many 'focal points', or you won't know where to look first.
- The following genera are some of the best choices for containers:

*Juniperus* (Juniper)
*Chamaecyparis* (False Cypress)
*Pinus* (Pine)
*Tsuga* (Hemlock)
*Abies* (Fir)
*Picea* (Spruce)

- Almost any conifer can be trained as a hedge. The easiest ones to use are those that shear very well and re-sprout on old wood, such as plants in the following three genera:

*Cephalotaxus* (Plum Yew)
*Taxus* (Yew)
*Thuja* (Arborvitae)

- Other conifers that tolerate shearing well but do not re-sprout on old wood include:

*Cupressocyparis Cupressus* (Cypress)
*Juniperus* (Juniper)
*Podocarpus Tsuga* (Hemlock)

- Cedars grow to a tremendous height, but there are beautiful bush varieties that have been developed for the small garden. Look out for forms that grow into a dense compact bush.

*Cedrus libani Nana* – a dwarf form of cedar to look out for. It grows into a dense bush no larger that 1 to 1.5 metres in height and width.

*Cedrus deodara Pendula,* – spreads flat on the ground, with the occasional branch-end feebly attempting to rise.

*Cypress* – *Chamaecyparis* – grown in many varieties. Some are large and others are dwarf forms. All are easy to grow and are suitable for a variety of purposes.

*Chamaecyparis Ellwoodii* – excellent for rock gardens; grey-green columnar tree; extremely slow-growing.

*Chamaecyparis Ellwood's Gold* – height 2 metres, width 45cm, is yellow-green in spring and early summer, darkening in late summer and winter. Lifting and replanting in the autumn can retard the growth further.

*Chamaecyparis lawsoniana Minima* and *Nana* – dwarf forms growing no more than 1.5 metres in height and width.

*Chamaecyparis lawsoniana Glauca* – a slender green-grey form. It grows to 1.5 to 2.5 metres high but is only 60cm wide.

*Chamaecyparis plumosa Aurea Nana* and *plumosa Pygmaea* – are compact bun-shaped forms that have beautiful golden foliage. Plant golden foliaged plants in sunny positions.

*Chamaecyparis squarrosa Compacta* and *squarrosa Nana* – have grey-green foliage.

- Junipers are the hardiest of the garden conifers. They can be columnar, irregular, some are spreading and some prostrate. The dwarf or slow-growing varieties are ideal for the modern garden.

*Juniperus chinensis Aurea* – slow-growing columnar tree growing to a height of 7 metres by 1.5 metres wide. Plant in a sunny spot of the garden where the leaves will shimmer gold in full light.

*Juniperus communis Compressa* – a slow-growing tree, ideal for the rock garden, growing to a height of 45cm.

*Juniperus Japonica, tricta, Globosa,* and *P it eriana* – prostrate varieties, which are very useful for ground cover.

*Juniperus hori ontalis oug lasii* – has blue-green foliage turning rich purple in autumn.

*Juniperus hori ontalis Glauca* – has rich blue-green foliage and long whip-like terminals.

- ❑ Yew can thrive in almost any garden soil, except very boggy sites. They tolerate deep shade or full sun. This is a useful tree for topiary.
- ❑ Plant yew cuttings between October and April. For hedges, use plants that are approximately 6 to 10cm high and place them about 30 to 45cm apart.
- ❑ All parts of the yew except for the flesh of the berries is poisonous, so never plant this tree next to grazing land.

*Taxus baccata Aurea* – attractive golden colour, slower growing than the dark green form but is worth the wait.

*Taxus baccata astigiata* – is an upright dense columnar form of dark green. There are golden forms in cultivation also.

*Picea abies* – is the traditional Christmas tree. There are many dwarf and slow-growing forms available. These conifers have some of the most remarkable and beautiful colours, especially in spring when the new foliage creates an exquisite background against the previous year's foliage.

*Picea pungens osteri, Picea pungens Thomsen, Picea pungens Moerheimi* – these varieties grow to a height of 7 to 8 metres with a spread of 3 metres.

*Picea abies Nidi ormis* – grows to a height of 30cm and a width of 1 metre.

*Picea pungens Glauca Pendula* – has an attractive pendulous habit. The young shoots being grey-blue or almost white, shading to a darker green-blue later in the year.

Pine trees are one of the most commonly grown.

*Pinus Mugo* – grows to about 5 metres in height and 2 to 5 metres in width. It has dark green needles and brown cones.

*Pumilio* – is a smaller form of *Pinus Mugo.* It is a dwarf mountain pine often grown in a prostate form.

Section 8

# The Vegetable Garden

Vegetables are grown in greater variety, of higher quality, and are harvested earlier and later in the season than ever considered possible by gardeners of former generations. Thus, a well-cared-for vegetable garden will amply reward you and your family with an abundance of nutritious vegetables to be enjoyed fresh or preserved for later use.

When planning your garden, choose a site that is exposed to the sun throughout the day, and if possible, located near a water supply. To make the most of the space available, beds should be used continuously by planting successive in-season crops, as soon as the last gathering of vegetables is done, by using the rotation crop method.

Prepare the soil in autumn by spreading a thick layer of compost over the beds, and allow the rain to wash the nutrients into the soil. Lightly fork the compost into the topsoil when dry weather permits. Hoe the garden as often as needed to control weeds and grasses, but don't hoe too deeply during the growing season, otherwise you could damage the roots of vegetables. Treat each variety of vegetable according to its own special cultural requirement, growth, space, and pest control. Water the garden as often as needed to maintain a uniform moisture supply. In the absence of rain, a good soaking once a week will probably be adequate for heavier soils. Light sandy soils might require an application more frequently. Water early in the morning so foliage will dry off quickly, which helps prevent disease.

Harvest at the proper stage of maturity to get the highest quality vegetables. If crops such as beans and cucumbers are left on the vine to mature, the plants will stop producing, so it is essential to pick vegetables regularly. Any surplus production should be frozen or bottled as soon as possible after harvesting.

**Asparagus** *(Asparagus officinalis)*

- Don't harvest a full crop of asparagus until the fourth year of growth. If you can't wait, a few spears may be cut in the second and third year of growth without detriment to the plant. After plants are well established, they will produce spears for 6 to 10 weeks.
- A careful clean-up of the beds should begin in the autumn, but don't cut down the top growth until they change colour, and then all the top growth may be cleared away.
- Asparagus is winter hardy, so mulching is not essential. Mulching, however, is beneficial for weed control and moisture retention.
- Some gardeners use salt as a weed-killer in asparagus beds. Nowadays, it's considered to be detrimental to the plant, and may prove destructive to the roots. For a time, the salt renders the bed cold, and when followed by snow or frost the two combine to make a freezing mixture which arrests the growth of established plants.
- In gardens near the coast, seaweed is the best fertiliser for asparagus.

**Runner Beans** *(Phaseolus multiflorus)*

- Prepare the soil well in advance of planting. In gardens where the soil is acid, spread lime in late winter to improve the soil balance and fertility.
- To improve the looks of your vegetable garden, plant runner beans in full sun at the base of sunflowers. They act like trellises and are a delight to look at!

- Harvest when pods are about 10cm long, and keep picking to maintain flower and bean production. Plants should produce a constant supply of beans throughout August and September.

**Dwarf Beans** *(Phaseolus vulgaris)*

- Dwarf types are preferable in very limited space, and where runner beans create too much shade for neighbouring crops. Dwarf beans can be spaced closer and will produce a greater quantity at any one time than a similar planting of runner beans.

**Beetroot** *(Beta vulgaris)*

- Don't apply too much nitrogen fertiliser, otherwise you will end up with excessive top growth and nothing below ground.
- Beetroot prefers a pH between 6.5 and 7, therefore, the addition of lime is necessary in many soils to grow the best crop.
- When growing beetroot save space and eliminate weeding by planting two rows 15cm apart. Your next two rows should be planted 25cm from the previous two rows. Continue with as many rows as you desire. This enables you to control weeds better, and space-saving and harvesting is made easier. Make sure to plant plenty of beetroot and pickle them.

**Broccoli** *(Brassica oleracea botrytis asparagoides)*

- Broccoli needs cool weather for the heads to form satisfactorily. As a rule, plants sown in April will make the best crops, although much depends on season, soil, and climate. Select an open breezy place for late sowing.
- Sprouting broccoli, both white and purple, are valuable sources of green vegetables in winter and early spring. The plants may be allowed to remain until the weather makes heads tough and poor tasting.

**Brussels Sprouts** *(Brassica oleracea bullata gemmifera)*

- ❑ Brussels sprouts take up valuable space throughout the summer and are only ready for picking in the autumn after the weather cools. During the growing season, plant a crop of French beans in between rows. When the sprouts need the room, cut down the French bean plants to a low level with a pair of shears, leaving the roots in the ground to provide extra nitrogen for the sprouts.
- ❑ When harvesting sprouts, cut them off the stalk, rather than by pulling. Start by removing sprouts from the bottom of the plant, and working your way to the top as the season progresses. Don't remove the top leaves when they turn yellow as they protect the sprouts forming below.

**Cabbage** *(Brassica oleraccea capitata)*

- ❑ If you start your seedlings off in the warmth of your house, move them to a hotbed or cold-frame as soon as germination begins. Seedlings left to grow in the house will become leggy, due to the higher temperature.
- ❑ Over-watering and heavy rains after heads are well developed often cause splitting. Prompt harvesting is therefore essential. If not possible, twist or pull the plant slightly to tear some of the roots and cut down on water absorption and consequent splitting. Some varieties are more prone to splitting.
- ❑ If your cabbages wilt in hot weather and recover when it's cool, it may be a sign that they have club-root. Guard against it by destroying affected seedlings, and dipping transplants in a solution of Thiophanate Methyl.
- ❑ Don't plant cabbage near strawberries, garlic, or peas, as they don't like each other.

**Carrot** *(daucus Carota)*

- ❑ Heavy soils, rocky soils, insufficient fertiliser, and crowding can lead to stubby short roots.

- Hot weather may stunt growth, but when followed by a period of wet favourable weather, roots may rapidly expand and develop cracks.
- Knobbly roots indicate that you have nematode problems.
- To prevent forking, never transplant seeding, and don't use manure or grow on stony soil.
- Carrot-fly will cause the leaves of carrots to wilt in the sun: spray with an insecticide to remedy the problem.
- Carrot-willow aphids will cause the leaves to become discoloured or twisted: spray with an insecticide as soon as aphids are seen.

**Cauliflower** *(Brassica oleracea botrytis cauliflora)*

- Too much light reaching the curd will cause it to take on a greenish hue. To prevent this happening tie the large leaves together over the curd to shade it from the light.
- Insufficient fertiliser and hot weather will cause the curd to taste bitter.
- Late planting produces less vigorous plants, thus impeding the growth of leaves that are required to shield the curd from bright sunshine.
- Cauliflowers that are ready but not wanted immediately may be left in the ground. Break the mid-ribs of two or three of the centre leaves on the head curd, and bend the leaves over so that they protect the curd until required.
- Harvest cauliflowers early in the morning, before the dew has time to dry.
- If you have too many cauliflowers ready at one time, pull them up, roots and all, and hang them up by the roots in a cool, dark place. Every evening spray the plants with water. They should remain good for at least a few weeks.

**Celery** *(Apium graveolens)*

- ❑ Avoid buying celery plants that are too large for their containers. They are likely to bolt before they can grow any edible stalks.
- ❑ When rotating crops, don't grow celery where plants from the *Brassica* family have been grown.
- ❑ Celery heart-rot is seen as pink spots and dying growth near the base of stalks.

**Cucumber** *(Cumimis sativus)*

- ❑ Insufficient watering may cause your cucumbers to taste bitter. Wide temperature fluctuations such as a sharp drop, also adds to the problem. Cucumber mosaic is another cause of bitter fruit.
- ❑ To increase the yield of cucumbers, nip out three rough leaves when they are young. This will encourage the production of shoots from the base. When the shoots have made four leaves, nip the points to promote a further growth of side shoots. After this there must be no more stopping until there is a show of fruit.
- ❑ Poor pollination is the main cause of misshapen fruit. Since cucumbers require cross-pollination, good bee activity is essential. Drought conditions, hot weather, bacterial wilt or cucumber mosaic may also lead to deformed fruit.
- ❑ Save space by training cucumber plants to grow on a wire cage. This keeps the cucumbers off the ground.

**Lettuce** *(Lactuca sativa)*

- ❑ Slow growth results in lettuce leaves being tough and leathery. Make sure your seedlings are not crowded, well watered, and planted on fertile ground.
- ❑ Late planting of lettuce and hot weather will stunt growth and reduce quality.

- Hot weather will cause lettuce to bolt and go to seed. Plant early and shade plants in very hot weather.
- By sowing thinly in boxes, and kept under glass, a dense growth is produced in a short time, which can be cut in the same manner as mustard. One of the best white Cos varieties should be sown, and the crop will make an excellent component of a salad at any season of the year.

**Onion** *(Allium Cepa)*

- When buying onion sets select bulbs no larger than 2cm in diameter. Larger bulbs have a greater tendency to run to seed in the garden.
- Allow the tops of onions to fall over naturally when the bulb has matured. Those that remain upright after maturity may be broken down to help close the necks. Onions that do not fall over naturally tend to be poor keepers and should be kept separate and used first.

**Peas** *(Pisum sativum)*

- Quite often pea plants will wilt in hot weather, so mulch between rows to keep the soil cool longer, and always use wilt resistant varieties.
- Peas are vulnerable to soil diseases, as a preventative measure rotate pea plantings to prevent build-up of soil diseases.
- Plant your peas early to get maximum growth and production before the hot weather arrives.
- Grow a few extra pea plants for seed only. The practise of keeping a few pods on plants that are being cropped will reduce the plants overall crop.

**Potato** *(Solanum tuberosum)*

- Very wet weather, poorly-drained soils or planting too deep may lead to the development of rhizoctonia or other diseases that rot the young shoots before they become established.

- Always plant certified seed potatoes. This means that the potatoes used for planting were inspected in the growing fields and are free from diseases that may be carried on the seed section.
- To stop potatoes from sprouting in storage, place them in a cool, dark place where the temperature is less than 5°C, but not below freezing point.
- Potatoes turn green when exposed to the light, and are toxic. Keep roots well covered with a thick layer of soil, or compost. If your potatoes have turned green, remove all the green portions before cooking. The green portion contains an alkaloid known as solanine, which can cause illness.

**Radish** *(Raphanus sativus)*

- Early planting and an adequate supply of water will prevent slow growth in hot weather, or dry seasons.
- Too much nitrogen in the soil or planting too late will cause the leaf to grow abundantly with little or no bulb below ground.

**Rhubarb** *(Rheum hybridum)*

- Poor growing conditions, drought and hot weather will stimulate your rhubarb to flower. Cut out the flower -stalks as soon as they are noticed to help prevent weakening the plant.
- Plant rhubarb in a sunny position. Too much shade will prevent rhubarb stalks from colouring up.
- In poorly-drained areas, rhubarb is subject to damage from one of the crown rot fungi. Damage may also result from stalk borers or rhubarb curculio.
- When fully exposed to the light, forced rhubarb has a full colour; but the quality is better, and the colour quite sufficient if it is forced in the dark.

**Spinach** *(Spinacia oleracea)*

- Spinach doesn't like acid soils, so if your garden is at all on the acid side, add lime to it before planting.

**Strawberries** *(Fragaria)*

- Remember not to take off too much straw when uncovering your strawberries in the spring. The extra straw left around the plant helps maintain moisture and assists in keeping weeds to a minimum.
- After you plant strawberries for the first year, pick off the blooms to make the plant healthy and make better and bigger strawberries for following years.

**Tomatoes** *(Lycopersicon esculentum. Solanaceae)*

- Fish emulsion (or simply water from your aquarium) applied when tomatoes are transplanted, and again when first blossoms appear obtain glorious results.
- When planting tomatoes add a couple of tablespoonfuls of Epsom salts to the soil; it will increase the plants fruit yield.
- Always remove new growth at the bottom of tomato plants. This will help reduce the chance of disease.
- To avoid blossom end-rot on tomatoes: crush the shells of 2 eggs in the hole of each young plant at the time of planting. This will add calcium to the plant throughout the growing season and stop bottom-rot.
- Too much nitrogen applied to plants early in the season before fruit production begins will cause too much foliage. Fertilise lightly when planting, and give a dressing of nitrogen after the fruit has begun to set.
- High temperatures will prevent fruit from developing. Night temperatures below 15°C and day temperatures above 32°C will stop flowers from setting fruit.

- Cold weather at time of fruit set may cause your tomatoes to become deformed. Varieties such as 'Beefsteak' type are more likely to have the problem.

**Turnip** *(Brassica Rapa)*

- Poor soil conditions or excess nitrogen at planting time may lead to turnips having poor root development. Another cause might be broadcasting seeds too thickly.
- Slow growth of the roots due to hot weather can result in poor quality roots. To overcome this problem plant turnips in a light soil, and water regularly.

## TIPS

- Always buy good-quality seed from a reputable company. Do not save your own seed unless it is a unique, unavailable variety.
- Poor seed germination is a result of unfavourable weather conditions at planting time. Soil should be well warmed before planting.
- Too much water in the soil, either due to heavy rains or poor drainage, reduces seed germination. Seedling diseases are especially destructive under excessively moist conditions.
- Other causes of poor germination include planting too deeply and crusting of the soil surface after heavy rains or careless watering. Mechanical injury to the seeds from insects, rodents or soil diseases may also cause poor germination.
- Seed that is old or improperly stored will germinate poorly or not at all.
- Whenever seeds germinate poorly, it is best to dig up and replant promptly, rather than to try to fill spaces with another sowing.
- Seeds sown in summer for an autumn crop (such as turnip and lettuce) may suffer from excessive heat and drying. When

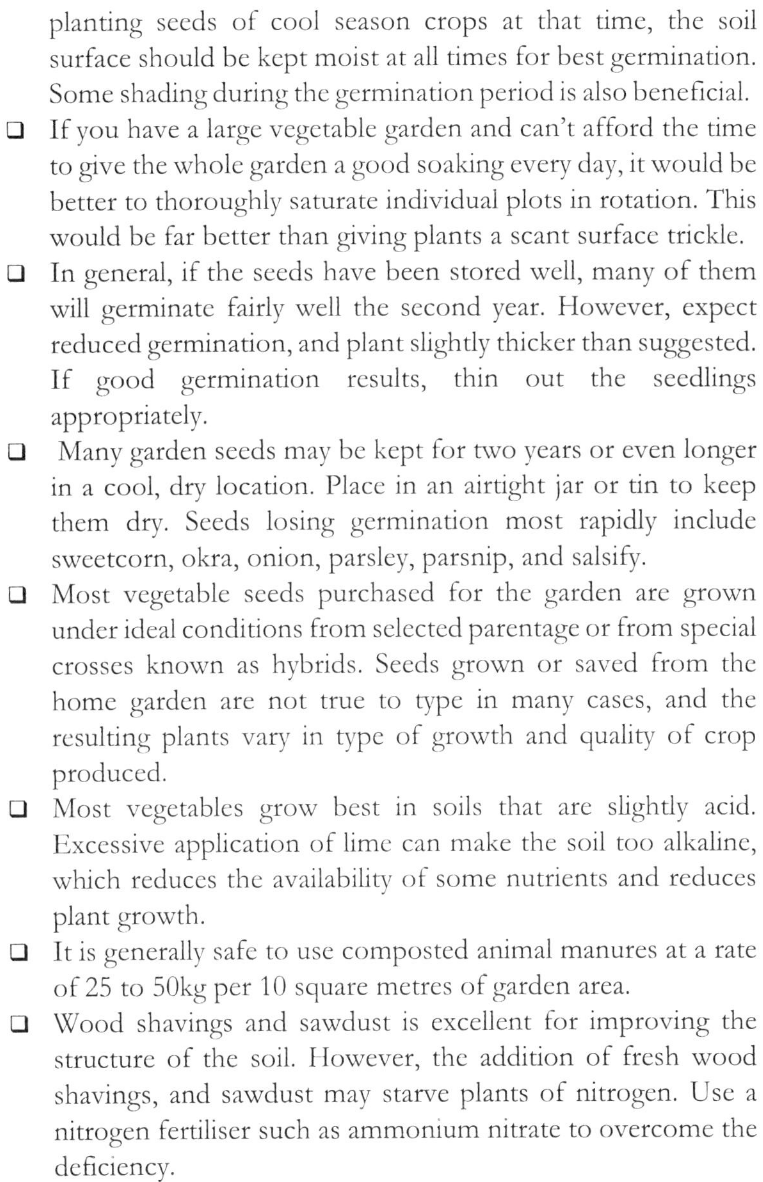

planting seeds of cool season crops at that time, the soil surface should be kept moist at all times for best germination. Some shading during the germination period is also beneficial.

- If you have a large vegetable garden and can't afford the time to give the whole garden a good soaking every day, it would be better to thoroughly saturate individual plots in rotation. This would be far better than giving plants a scant surface trickle.
- In general, if the seeds have been stored well, many of them will germinate fairly well the second year. However, expect reduced germination, and plant slightly thicker than suggested. If good germination results, thin out the seedlings appropriately.
- Many garden seeds may be kept for two years or even longer in a cool, dry location. Place in an airtight jar or tin to keep them dry. Seeds losing germination most rapidly include sweetcorn, okra, onion, parsley, parsnip, and salsify.
- Most vegetable seeds purchased for the garden are grown under ideal conditions from selected parentage or from special crosses known as hybrids. Seeds grown or saved from the home garden are not true to type in many cases, and the resulting plants vary in type of growth and quality of crop produced.
- Most vegetables grow best in soils that are slightly acid. Excessive application of lime can make the soil too alkaline, which reduces the availability of some nutrients and reduces plant growth.
- It is generally safe to use composted animal manures at a rate of 25 to 50kg per 10 square metres of garden area.
- Wood shavings and sawdust is excellent for improving the structure of the soil. However, the addition of fresh wood shavings, and sawdust may starve plants of nitrogen. Use a nitrogen fertiliser such as ammonium nitrate to overcome the deficiency.

- For most efficient use of water, it is best to water the garden in the early morning or late afternoon, but early enough so that the leaves will be dried thoroughly before dark. Watering in late evening or at night promotes the development of some diseases.
- Tall-growing plants should be grown together on the north or west-side of the garden so they won't shade lower-growing plants. The soil should have a good texture, and be fertile and well-drained.
- Use known or recommended cultivars for your main planting. Many other cultivars are available, and new cultivars are being introduced each year. Try a few new cultivars on a small scale to determine their worth in your area.
- When buying plants, insist on fresh, stocky plants that are free of diseases and nematodes.
- Grow super tomatoes by adding half a cup of skimmed milk added to 'All-Season Tonic', it provides an excellent spray tonic for tomatoes.

## HOME RECIPES FOR VEGETABLE GARDEN TREATMENTS

### Soil Conditioning Tonic

*Ingredients:*
10kg organic garden compost
450g sugar
200g Epsom salts
*Method:*
Mix ingredients and apply using a hand-held broadcast spreader on a medium setting.

### All-Season Conditioner

*Ingredients:*
1 can of beer

1 cup of washing-up liquid
1 cup of antiseptic mouthwash
¼ tsp instant tea granules
*Method:*
Combine ingredients in a 100-litre water barrel, topping the balance of the sprayer with regular cola. Over-spray the soil everywhere in your vegetable garden.

**All-Season Tonic**
*Ingredients:*
1 can of beer
1 cup of ammonia
1/2 cup of washing-up liquid
1/2 cup of liquid lawn food
1/2 cup of molasses
*Method:*
Mix ingredients and place in a 100-litre water barrel, and fill with water. Use to feed soil every three weeks during the growing season. Spray in the mornings.

**Insect and Disease Chaser**
*Ingredients:*
1 cup of children's shampoo
1 cup of chewing tobacco juice
1 cup of antiseptic mouthwash
*Method:*
Combine the ingredients in 100-litre water barrel, and fill with water. Use to bathe the garden every two weeks during the growing season. Dispense in the evenings for greater effect.

**Autumn Clean-Up Tonic**
Clean your garden at the end of the season and over-spray with this fantastic tonic.

*Ingredients:*
1 can of beer
1 can of regular cola
1/2 cup of washing-up liquid
1/2 cup of chewing tobacco juice
*Method:*
Combine ingredients in 100-litre water barrel, and fill with water. Use to treat the entire garden.

**Late Autumn Tonic**
*Ingredients:*
1 can of regular cola
1 cup of washing-up liquid
¼ cup of ammonia
*Method:*
Combine ingredients in a 100-litre water barrel, and fill with water. Cover the garden first in grass cuttings and leaves. Over-spray with the tonic, then fork into the soil, and leave to over-winter.

## SECTION 9

# Growing And Storing Herbs

Herbs grown for their pot-pourri, culinary, medicinal and ornamental uses play an important part in our lives. They range from plants grown annually from seed, such as basil, to more permanent perennials, such as tarragon, rosemary, lavender, and bay.

Traditionally, herbs have been grown in special formal gardens all by themselves. They will, however, grow quite happily in a mixed border or vegetable plot, but tend to grow better when grouped together to make an interesting section of your garden. Lavender and rosemary can be planted as low hedging; others such as ornamental sage can be part of a mixed planting. Bay can be grown as an evergreen and trimmed or shaped. Plants such as lavender and rosemary have aromatic foliage and many herbs are suited for drying for later use.

Herbs are very versatile and can be grown in as big or as small an area as you can manage. Even a small tub or window-box can give instant access to fresh herbs all year long. Most herbs like sunshine, so a sunny spot is ideal. If you make sure there are no tall or overhanging hedges or trees creating shade you should be successful in providing all the herbs you require.

### SOWING AND PLANTING

Herbs grown from seed should be sown in the spring in a greenhouse or on a window-sill. This means you can get a head start, but protect the young seedlings from frost and slugs. As soon as they are large enough, plant in pots and then harden off before planting out in late spring.

Any good, well-drained soil in full sun will work well for most herbs. Only a few herbs require any shade. Limit your use of fertiliser as most herbs have better flavour and aroma with lower fertility levels. Cultivate the soil to a depth of 30cm and improve heavy clay soil with sand or sphagnum peat to improve drainage. Herbs are annual, biennial, or perennial, and it is a good idea to label the plants accordingly so that you will know which ones to replace each year.

## TIPS

- ❑ Perennial herbs that you've grown and harvested throughout the summer months may need a little additional care to keep them growing well into the autumn. Lavender, sage, hyssop, and rosemary appreciate a little lime scratched into the soil around the base of the plants to keep the soil on the sweet side.
- ❑ Fuzzy-leafed foliage herbs such as artemisia and horehound rot easily if their foliage is wet, so bottom water these herbs.
- ❑ Pinch back herbs such as scented geraniums to make the plants bush out, and prune others such as catmint to half the plant's original size to force new shoots and flowers for autumn.
- ❑ Many herbs such as chives, thyme, sage, fennel and lavender are winter hardy and will survive the winter best left in the ground.
- ❑ Some short-lived herbs such as basil are treated as annuals and should be allowed to perish with the frost, mainly because they are old and will not last much longer anyway.
- ❑ Biennials such as parsley are generally left in place so that they may grow again next year, set seed, and perpetuate themselves in a little patch.
- ❑ Tropical plants used as herbs such as scented geraniums and

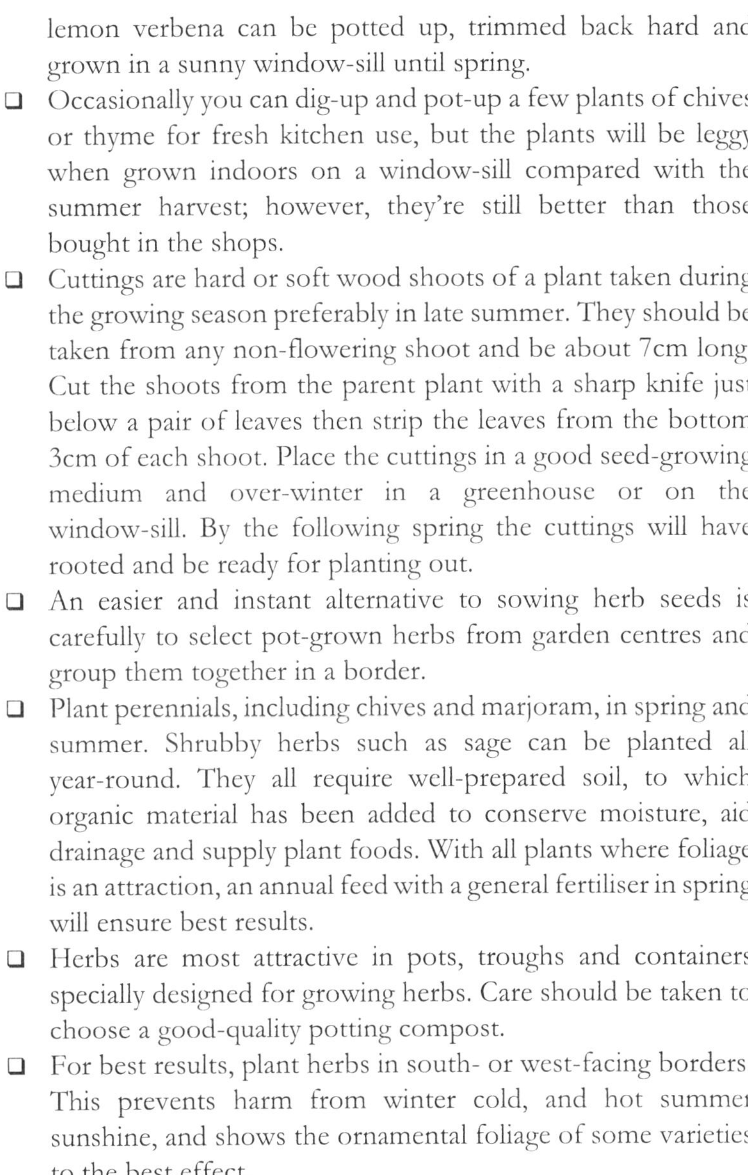

lemon verbena can be potted up, trimmed back hard and grown in a sunny window-sill until spring.

- Occasionally you can dig-up and pot-up a few plants of chives or thyme for fresh kitchen use, but the plants will be leggy when grown indoors on a window-sill compared with the summer harvest; however, they're still better than those bought in the shops.
- Cuttings are hard or soft wood shoots of a plant taken during the growing season preferably in late summer. They should be taken from any non-flowering shoot and be about 7cm long. Cut the shoots from the parent plant with a sharp knife just below a pair of leaves then strip the leaves from the bottom 3cm of each shoot. Place the cuttings in a good seed-growing medium and over-winter in a greenhouse or on the window-sill. By the following spring the cuttings will have rooted and be ready for planting out.
- An easier and instant alternative to sowing herb seeds is carefully to select pot-grown herbs from garden centres and group them together in a border.
- Plant perennials, including chives and marjoram, in spring and summer. Shrubby herbs such as sage can be planted all year-round. They all require well-prepared soil, to which organic material has been added to conserve moisture, aid drainage and supply plant foods. With all plants where foliage is an attraction, an annual feed with a general fertiliser in spring will ensure best results.
- Herbs are most attractive in pots, troughs and containers specially designed for growing herbs. Care should be taken to choose a good-quality potting compost.
- For best results, plant herbs in south- or west-facing borders. This prevents harm from winter cold, and hot summer sunshine, and shows the ornamental foliage of some varieties to the best effect.

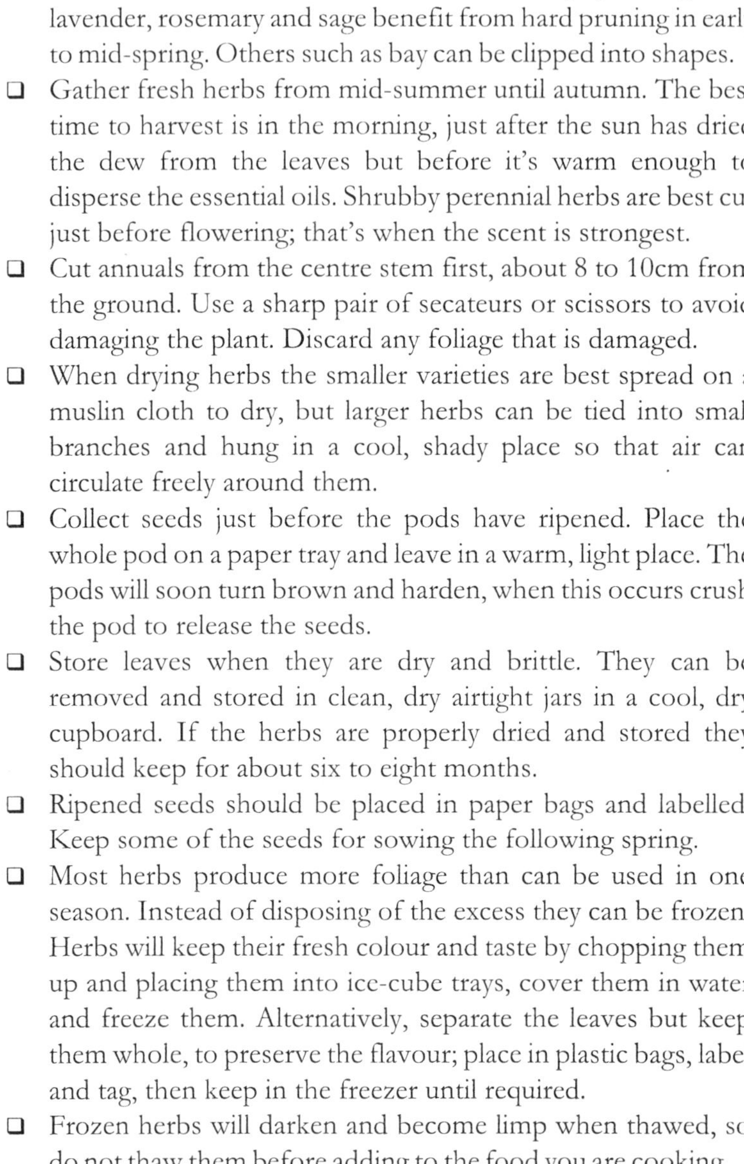

- Herbs such as cotton lavender, the curry plant, garden lavender, rosemary and sage benefit from hard pruning in early to mid-spring. Others such as bay can be clipped into shapes.
- Gather fresh herbs from mid-summer until autumn. The best time to harvest is in the morning, just after the sun has dried the dew from the leaves but before it's warm enough to disperse the essential oils. Shrubby perennial herbs are best cut just before flowering; that's when the scent is strongest.
- Cut annuals from the centre stem first, about 8 to 10cm from the ground. Use a sharp pair of secateurs or scissors to avoid damaging the plant. Discard any foliage that is damaged.
- When drying herbs the smaller varieties are best spread on a muslin cloth to dry, but larger herbs can be tied into small branches and hung in a cool, shady place so that air can circulate freely around them.
- Collect seeds just before the pods have ripened. Place the whole pod on a paper tray and leave in a warm, light place. The pods will soon turn brown and harden, when this occurs crush the pod to release the seeds.
- Store leaves when they are dry and brittle. They can be removed and stored in clean, dry airtight jars in a cool, dry cupboard. If the herbs are properly dried and stored they should keep for about six to eight months.
- Ripened seeds should be placed in paper bags and labelled. Keep some of the seeds for sowing the following spring.
- Most herbs produce more foliage than can be used in one season. Instead of disposing of the excess they can be frozen. Herbs will keep their fresh colour and taste by chopping them up and placing them into ice-cube trays, cover them in water and freeze them. Alternatively, separate the leaves but keep them whole, to preserve the flavour; place in plastic bags, label and tag, then keep in the freezer until required.
- Frozen herbs will darken and become limp when thawed, so do not thaw them before adding to the food you are cooking.

- Herbs that prefer full sun are basil, chives, dill, oregano, rosemary, tarragon, and thyme. Partial shade-loving herbs are chervil, lemon balm, and mint.
- To chop parsley, basil or sage, use a chef's knife, and holding down the tip end of the herb, cut back and forth across whole pieces.
- To chop herbs, place the leaves in a glass measuring cup or small bowl, and cut them into tiny pieces with kitchen shears using short, quick strokes.
- To add a bit of colour to pasta or rice, sprinkle snipped basil leaves over the top after cooking.
- Crown an omelette with chive spears.
- Lay feathery tarragon or cilantro on a bowl of creamy dip.
- Decorate desserts with a sprig of mint.
- To select commercially-grown herbs, choose plants that are not yet in flower, but are a rich colour, with no dark spots on the leaves.
- To substitute fresh herbs for dried herbs in recipes, use 1 tablespoonful of fresh herbs to replace 1 teaspoonful of dried herbs.
- The peak season for most herbs is July through to September. Most can be found in the produce section of the supermarket.
- Plant mint in a plastic bucket with the bottom cut off. This will stop the mint from spreading.
- Plant mint around your walkways in your garden. Then when you step on it or brush past it when walking through it smells great.

## Section 10

# Fruit From Your Garden

Almost any kind of fruit can be grown in the home garden; even the smallest garden can produce soft fruits such as raspberries, which take up very little ground space. Hedges can be created with blackcurrant bushes, and bare walls can be covered with blackberries and fruit trees. And they're all very pleasing to the eye.

There are many different types of viruses that seriously attack fruit-bearing plants, so always buy your plants from an approved stockist. Look for plants that are young and green, and ignore those that have been hanging around in the nursery for some years, as they are apt to be pot-bound, and will inevitably produce stunted trees due to the roots having insufficient room to develop.

### Cherry

These hardy deciduous trees are grown for their edible, single-seeded fruits. Cherry trees grow on almost every kind of soil, so long as it is well-drained. Plant in open ground, away from areas where the blossom can be caught by late frosts. Cherry trees are susceptible to cherry leaf spot, and brown rot. Birds are the main problem and may devour an entire crop if precautions are not taken. Too much rain when the fruit ripens can cause splitting or cracking, making the fruit inedible.

### Quince

The best time for planting quince trees is during late October or November. Plant your trees in a loamy, moist soil, preferably near water. In very small gardens, quince trees can be trained on an espalier, or on a sheltered wall or fence. The common quince is a self-fertile, small tree with flowers forming on the end of new growth in the spring. The fruits generally ripen outdoors, but only in southern areas where the weather is warmer. Gather the fruits in October before the threat of cold frosts at night. Most fruits weigh up to 450g, and are very hard, suitable only in preserves. Drooping branches may need to be shortened. Little pruning is needed on mature trees except for removing water-suckers.

### Apple

Plant bare rooted apple trees in November whilst the ground is still warm enough to give the plants a head start for the following year's growth. Plant container-grown trees at any time, except when the ground is frozen. The most suitable garden soil to grow apple trees is where there is deep soil ranging in texture from a sandy loam to a sandy clay loam. Apple trees blossom best in sheltered areas where they are not exposed to cold winds and early frosts. Trees planted under favourable conditions will set more fruit than they are capable of successfully carrying to maturity, so the removal of excess fruit is essential to assure satisfactory development. Failure to remove the excess fruit will decrease the amount of blossom forming the following year, and cause the tree to only produce a crop every other year. Excess fruit should be removed by hand, reducing the apples to one per cluster with fruiting clusters spaced about every 15cm along the branch. The earlier that hand-thinning is completed, the more effective it will be in achieving good-quality fruits.

If the apples are ripe they can be removed easily when lifted and twisted slightly. Early varieties should be harvested just before they ripen. Late varieties will not ripen on the tree; these should be collected before the strong autumn winds begin to blow them off the tree.

### Pear

Plant pear trees in the autumn before the ground begins to cool. Certain varieties of pears are self-pollinating, thus, if you want only one pear tree, a self-pollinating variety should be selected. Best results will be obtained by planting on well-drained, deep soil that doesn't dry out in the summer. Watering may be required to help new trees to become established.

To obtain high-quality fruit, pears must be harvested before they are ripe; but not too early, otherwise they will be undersized and lack sweetness and flavour. If picked too late, the fruit will quickly ripen, becoming gritty in texture, and the core turning pappy and brown.

Store pears for ripening in single layers, unwrapped on trays, in a cool room. The temperature should preferably be around 2 to 4°C. Check frequently and remove pears that are ready for eating.

### Plum

Plum trees are usually taken from cuttings and grafted onto a rootstock so that the variety of plum runs true to its genus. Most plum trees are not self-pollinating, so before buying check out your local neighbourhood to see if there are any other plum trees in the vicinity. If not, then it may be necessary to have more than one variety of plum tree in your garden.

Because plum trees are early flowering, they should be grown in sheltered positions to protect the blossom from cold wind and frost.

Plum trees will set more fruit than the trees are capable of successfully carrying to maturity. Therefore, the removal of excess fruit from the tree is essential to ensure satisfactory development of the crop. Excess fruit should be removed by hand so that the remaining fruit is spaced about 15cm apart. The earlier hand-thinning is completed, the more effective it will be in achieving the desired results.

### Strawberry

Always buy healthy young plants from a nursery that sells

certified virus-free plants. To get a strawberry bed started, they should be planted during the months of August and September. Plant in an area that receives full sun for most of the day, and where the soil is light with good drainage. Make sure that all weeds are removed before planting, and a generous amount of compost dug into the topsoil to get them off to a good start.

Shortly after planting, begin removing any flowers that may appear until the spring of the first year to allow the plants to develop. During the first summer, allow the strawberry runners to develop. Since strawberries are surface-rooting plants don't hoe too deeply between plants, as the roots can easily be damaged. To prevent slug damage and to keep fruits off the soil, mulch with generous amounts of meadow hay, or polythene strips.

**Blackberry**

The well-known blackberry, grown largely for its fruit, grows wild in most parts of Great Britain. It is a native of many parts of Europe. The stems are erect and shrubby, biennial, with creeping perennial roots. It flowers in May and June. Planting in the fruit garden can take place at any time between October and March. They will grow quite satisfactorily in any sunny spot in soils ranging from sand to clay, but do best on sandy loam or clay loam soils.

The best time to harvest berries is early in the morning when the dew has begun to dry, and before the birds steal the ripening fruits. Because fruit ripens very quickly, another check for ripened fruit should be made in the evening. Fruits are at their peak of ripeness when they lose their high glossy shine and turn slightly dull.

Water blackberries during dry weather. Apply liberally so that the water reaches down to the roots below the ground surface. Mulching will help to conserve moisture.

**Raspberry**

New plants are generally propagated by suckers, though those raised from layers should be preferred, because they will be better rooted and not so liable to send out more suckers. In preparing these plants, canes should be shortened, but the buds that are placed at a small distance from the stem of the plant must not be cut off, as they produce the new shoots the following summer. Place the plants about 60cm apart in rows, allowing 1 metre between the rows. If planted too closely, without plenty of air between the rows, the fruit will not be so fine.

The most suitable soil is a good, strong loam. In October, cut down all the old wood that has produced fruit in the summer and shorten the young shoots to about 60cm in length. Dig the spaces between the rows well and dress with a little manure. Beyond weeding during the summer, no further care is needed. It is wise to form new beds every three or four years, as the fruit on old plants is apt to deteriorate.

### Redcurrant and Blackcurrant

These are shrubby bush plants that bear colourful spring flowers and abundant berries that are tasty when processed. They do well on almost any soil of average fertility. They can grow on soil that has poor drainage and will do well in partial shade.

*Varieties:*

Redcurrant – Red Lake, Perfection, and Wilder

Blackcurrant – Consort and Crusader

Plants may be grown singly or in hedgerows. Plant dormant stock when available for late winter planting, with the plants 1.5 metres apart. Mulch the soil because of the shallow root system. Prune to maintain vigorous fruiting on two-, three-, or four-year old wood. Old plants should be cut back to ground level to extend their fruiting capability.

### Gooseberry

Gooseberries are hardy plants, consequently, they perform better when they are grown in shaded parts of the fruit garden. Gooseberries do best in fertile, loamy soil that has been mulched, and has good drainage. They are low-growing deciduous shrubs that reach 1 to 1.5 metres in height and have thorny stems. They can be used in fruit gardens as well as in the flower garden borders. They are grown on a large scale commercially for their fruit, which is fresh-frozen or processed for use in jams and pies. Gooseberries contain several minerals and are high in vitamins A, B and C. There are several different varieties that have either green-, yellow-, red- or pink-coloured fruit. They may also have fine hairs on the skins.

## TIPS

- Most fruit trees require at least two varieties for cross-pollination in order to get a good crop of fruit.
- When buying fruit trees, look out for dwarf and semi-dwarf rootstocks, which are available for most fruit trees. Dwarf trees will grow to be 2.5 to 5m tall. Semi-dwarf trees will grow 4 to 7m tall. Pruning makes a big difference in size. Semi-dwarf trees are usually stronger and bear fruit sooner than dwarf trees.
- The first five years are the most important for training a fruit tree. So once your fruit trees have established themselves, they should be trained to have a single, upright trunk with well-spaced, spreading side branches.
- Apples, pears, and plums bear fruit on fruit spurs, which are short twigs on older wood. Spurs will die out if they are shaded too much. Upper and outer branches should be thinned out and cut back to let light and air into the centre of the tree.
- Suckers and water-sprouts grow rapidly straight up. They don't produce fruit, and shade out the spreading branches that do produce fruit. They can be plucked off when they first appear in June, which is much easier than cutting them off later. On the other hand, they can be tied down so that they grow outward and become productive branches.

- Fruit will have the most flavour if it is allowed to ripen on the tree and eaten right away, but will store longer if it is picked before it is fully ripe.
- To harvest fruit easily without bruising or damaging it, put your thumb next to the stem and wrap your fingers around the fruit. Lift and rotate the fruit so the stem is bent. If the fruit stem doesn't separate easily from the tree, the fruit is unripe.
- If you get too many birds in your garden, protect soft fruits with a wire netting cage, as large as necessary to cover the plants.
- When planting against brick or stone walls, take into account that the wall itself will extract moisture from the ground, and the soil will be dry at its foundations. To overcome this, bury upright a 5cm diameter drainpipe about 30cm away from each tree and pour water into the pipe whenever the weather conditions are extra dry.
- In large gardens, fruit should be grown in the higher parts of the garden, away from any frost pockets, and where they are in open ground to receive full sunlight and plenty of fresh air.

SECTION 11

# Greenhouse Gardening

Before choosing your new greenhouse, consider the space you have available, and how you intend using it. Space in your greenhouse is at a premium during spring and summer, so buy the largest one you can afford that will fit the space available.

## CHOOSING A SUITABLE SITE

If possible, locate the greenhouse where it will receive at least six hours of direct sunlight during the winter months. Select a flat, level site on free-draining soil, sheltered from high winds, close to water and electricity, and easily accessible from your home and garden. Avoid a site that is cold, has frost pockets, near children's play areas, or shaded by trees or buildings during the winter.

The best orientation is to position the greenhouse with its length running east and west. This will provide more heat gain from the sun during the winter. If the southern exposure is restricted, but open to the east, southeast, southwest, or west, turn the greenhouse to the winter sun. Remember that the sun is much lower during winter.

## BUILDING YOUR GREENHOUSE

Start off by laying the greenhouse foundation. The foundations must be square and level. Remove plants and grass, then level the site using a contractor's level. Square the foundation by measuring diagonally from opposite corners and shifting the frame until the measurements are equal.

## GREENHOUSE FLOOR

If you have not poured a concrete slab, you will need a walkway down the middle of your greenhouse. For an aisle of bricks: frame the walkway with 5 x 10cm treated timber, lay down 5cm of crushed hard core, then 5cm of sand, and set the bricks with 1.5cm spacing. A final touch is to plant lemon thyme between the bricks. Finish the remainder of the floor with 5cm of pea gravel.

## EQUIPPING THE GREENHOUSE

Place staging along one side of the greenhouse to provide a flat working surface, and the necessary space for trays and pots of seedlings. Line gravel trays to a depth of 2.5cm with capillary matting and then place on the staging.

## VENTILATION

It's essential to have good ventilation to prevent damping-off. This disease is seen as a grey mould found on the stems and leaves of you new plants and seedlings. If it should be present, treat it with a fungicide.

The best way to ensure good ventilation is to install automatic window and louvre openers. These operate by responding to temperature changes and will ensure that the plants get neither to hot nor too cold.

## HEATING

Heating is not essential but does allow you to keep tender plants in the greenhouse through the winter, and helps speed up growth of young plants in the spring. Paraffin heaters are ideal because as well as heat, they produce water vapour and carbon dioxide, which is also needed by plants.

## SHADING

Roof shading is a basic requirement for greenhouse temperature control during summer. Shading can greatly reduce overheating and help create a pleasant environment for both you and your plants! Shading also prevents sunburn of sensitive foliage.

Shade material should ideally be placed on the outside of the greenhouse, and suspended about 10cm above the glazing surface to allow air circulation. Shading installed inside the greenhouse will be 40% less effective. Inside shading will protect the plants from sunburn, but because of the 'greenhouse effect' the sun's energy is trapped in the greenhouse and overheating can result.

### Shade material

Black polythene has been a widely used shade material for many years. It is very durable and is available in a wide range of densities. The dark green latheing pattern is more attractive for residential greenhouses. This material does not roll up easily, however.

New knitted plastic shades are gaining in popularity because they are lightweight and easy to handle. They do roll up easily and don't unravel when cut to size.

The roll-up shade is simple in design and operation, very much like the common bamboo window-shades. The lines to control the shade are run through pulleys and can be controlled from either outside or inside the greenhouse.

During late autumn or early winter take down or remove greenhouse shading such as external slatted blinds. It is a good idea to take out capillary matting to reduce the internal humidity during winter months, since grey moulds will thrive in cool but humid conditions. Another precaution is to regularly remove dead material and ensure that you leave some space between plants to aid in airflow.

For really delicate plants, it is a good idea to put an insulated cold-frame inside the greenhouse, covered with a layer of bubble wrap or similar.

## CLEANING THE GREENHOUSE

Take all plants out of the greenhouse and thoroughly clean the frame, glazing, and benches with an effective disinfectant. Make glass sparkle brightly again with an effective cleaning detergent. Fibreglass and polycarbonate should be rinsed with a mild washing-up liquid and lukewarm water. Use a soft cloth or sponge. For polycarbonate, rub only in the same direction as the channels to avoid scratches that show. Metal frames, door hinges and vents should be oiled.

Replace any broken glass or ageing polycarbonate cover. Caulk as necessary, especially around the foundation. Apply foam tapes to doors and vents to make an airtight seal.

If you have single-layer glass and plan to heat your greenhouse, bubble insulation can provide significant heat savings. Simply apply to the inside of the walls and roof.

## TIPS

- During summer months, plants will be growing faster and soils will dry out quicker. Check plants in the morning and evening, keeping them well-watered to avoid dry root problems.
- Hose down the floor of the greenhouse and staging in the morning and early afternoon daily, to keep the atmosphere cooler and more humid.
- Plants coming into flower need high potash, as do tomatoes,

cucumbers and fruit. Occasionally water with clear water to flush out excess fertiliser salts.

- ❑ Be on the alert for pests! Whitefly, aphids, red spider, thrips and fungal diseases need to be controlled at first sight before they multiply! Make a regular, thorough check. Shake the plants and look under the leaves.
- ❑ Keep your greenhouse CLEAN. Remove all plant debris – faded flowers, yellowed leaves, etc.
- ❑ Train climbing vegetables up lattices, stakes, and strings.
- ❑ Many of the plants you started since autumn of last year will now be planted outside. Now you can use the extra space in your greenhouse to regenerate house-plants and ornamentals.
- ❑ For healthy green peppers in the greenhouse, sprinkle a little Epsom salts in a circle around the base of the peppers.
- ❑ Planting tomatoes in a greenhouse is a good idea, but you'll have to watch the air temperature closely. Tomatoes grow best at daily average temperatures of 18 to 24°C, and stop growing at temperatures above 35°C, and below 12°C. Prolonged exposure to temperatures below 10°C will kill the plants. Day temperatures above 32°C, and night temperatures above 22°C during bloom reduce fruit set. There is now considerable evidence to show that night temperatures are the most critical for best fruit production, with a range of 15 to 20°C giving you the best fruit set. So keep a close eye on the temperature inside your greenhouse and raise or lower the plastic accordingly.

## SECTION 12

# Digging And Weeding

It is generally regarded that October is the beginning of a new year in the garden. That is when the fruit and vegetable harvests are over, and summer annuals and perennial flowers cease to bloom. This is the time of year when foliage begins to turn brown and die-back occurs. Now is the time to make a start by clearing the garden plots of their spent crops and also of weeds. The opportunity should be taken to trim back surrounding hedges, the hedge clippings being placed on the compost heap, or burned with the resulting ashes being dug into the ground.

### THE KITCHEN GARDEN

Autumn is a time when you should give vacant plots in the kitchen garden a 'rough digging'. With most types of soil the work is best done with a spade, which should have a long, sharp blade with a square edge. For rough digging the clods are not broken up, hence the name, but are left just as they fall from the spade.

When ground has been 'rough dug', which is either in October or November, far more of its surface is exposed than would be the case if it were broken down to a fine tilth. This means that the soil is left completely open to cold frosts, which will break down the hard clods of tacky soil, and will also allow garden birds to more readily reach the pests and their eggs. Immediately the rough digging has been completed, the whole plot may be top-dressed with garden lime. Use up to about 150g to the square metre of surface. This liming is recommended every second autumn with almost all types of soil.

Rough digging in the autumn prepares the ground for spring sowing and planting, it should therefore remain in its broken condition throughout the winter months. As spring approaches it may be finally prepared by means of a further digging with a light forking over, and a top dressing of compost applied.

The flower garden is treated differently to the vegetable garden, because there are still perennials and shrubs in the beds throughout the winter months. Summer planting of annuals will usually die after the first frosts. Dig them up as soon as this happens and place them on the compost heap. At the same time, remove all weeds that are still flourishing. Any vacant ground should be given a light forking over. Be careful not to disturb plant roots and spring flowering bulbs that are now preparing to emerge from underground.

There are many plants that can be planted in the autumn that will look good on cold, cloudy days. Try winter-flowering pansies, polyanthus, primula, and violas. After planting, mulch the surface to a depth of 5cm between plants with a layer of compost: this will help to keep the soil warm during the cold months ahead, and will add nutrients to the soil, giving the plants a head start.

## TIPS

- ❑ Coping with weeds is the most time-consuming, laborious and never-ending problem for most gardeners. This need not be so, and coping with weeds before, or just as they make their appearance, when they are at their most vulnerable, is a useful guard against heavy weeding, if weeding is necessary at all.
- ❑ Weed control should start in the late summer and be monitored throughout the winter, so that you can start the new season with a clean garden. Don't worry too much about killing weeds before they make an appearance, however, as

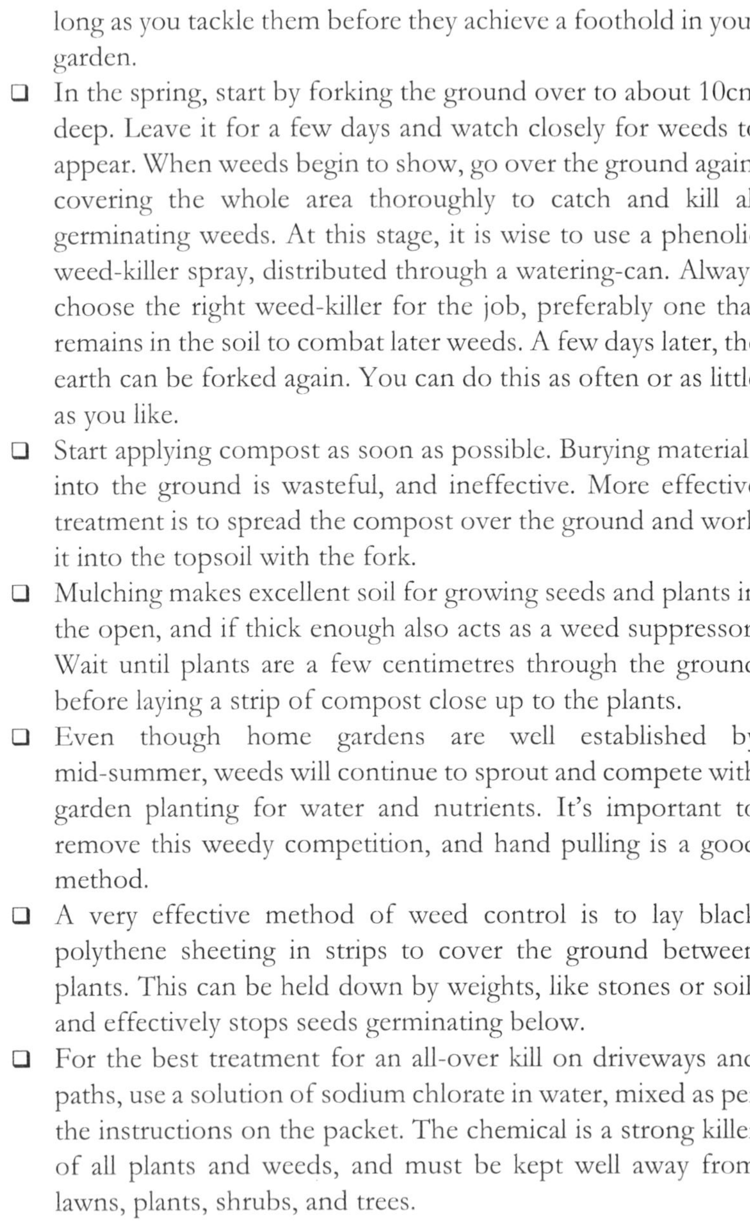

long as you tackle them before they achieve a foothold in your garden.

- In the spring, start by forking the ground over to about 10cm deep. Leave it for a few days and watch closely for weeds to appear. When weeds begin to show, go over the ground again, covering the whole area thoroughly to catch and kill all germinating weeds. At this stage, it is wise to use a phenolic weed-killer spray, distributed through a watering-can. Always choose the right weed-killer for the job, preferably one that remains in the soil to combat later weeds. A few days later, the earth can be forked again. You can do this as often or as little as you like.
- Start applying compost as soon as possible. Burying materials into the ground is wasteful, and ineffective. More effective treatment is to spread the compost over the ground and work it into the topsoil with the fork.
- Mulching makes excellent soil for growing seeds and plants in the open, and if thick enough also acts as a weed suppressor. Wait until plants are a few centimetres through the ground before laying a strip of compost close up to the plants.
- Even though home gardens are well established by mid-summer, weeds will continue to sprout and compete with garden planting for water and nutrients. It's important to remove this weedy competition, and hand pulling is a good method.
- A very effective method of weed control is to lay black polythene sheeting in strips to cover the ground between plants. This can be held down by weights, like stones or soil, and effectively stops seeds germinating below.
- For the best treatment for an all-over kill on driveways and paths, use a solution of sodium chlorate in water, mixed as per the instructions on the packet. The chemical is a strong killer of all plants and weeds, and must be kept well away from lawns, plants, shrubs, and trees.

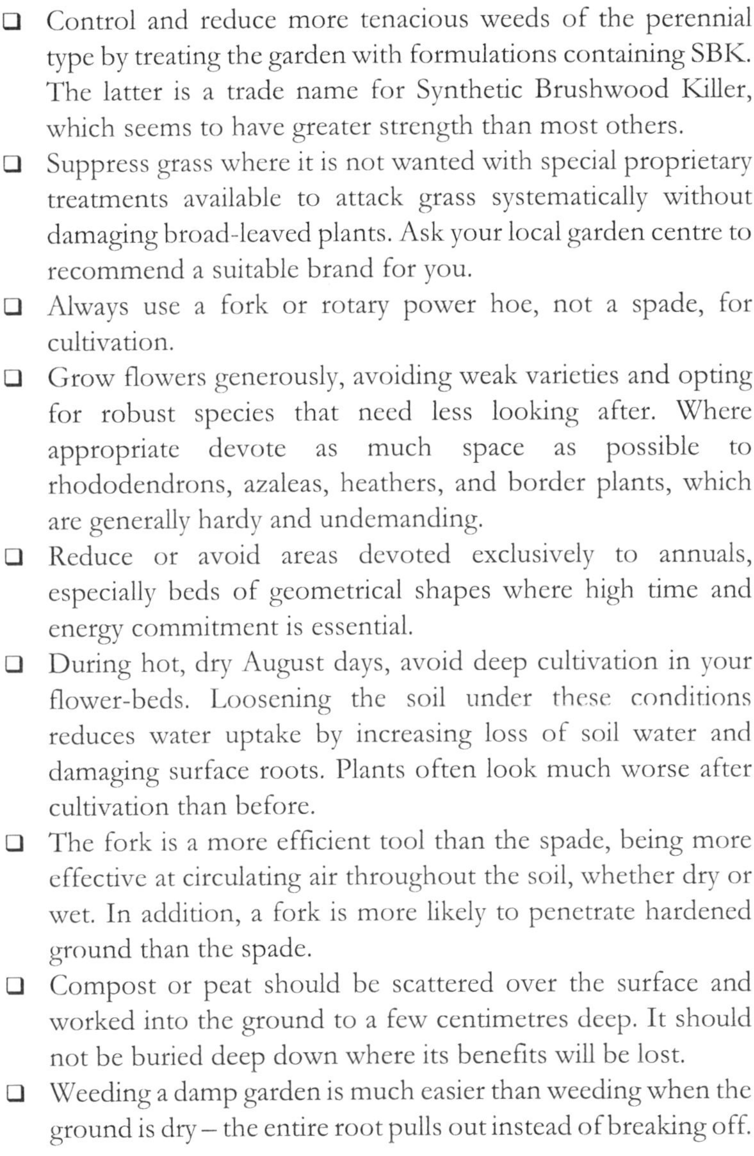

- Control and reduce more tenacious weeds of the perennial type by treating the garden with formulations containing SBK. The latter is a trade name for Synthetic Brushwood Killer, which seems to have greater strength than most others.
- Suppress grass where it is not wanted with special proprietary treatments available to attack grass systematically without damaging broad-leaved plants. Ask your local garden centre to recommend a suitable brand for you.
- Always use a fork or rotary power hoe, not a spade, for cultivation.
- Grow flowers generously, avoiding weak varieties and opting for robust species that need less looking after. Where appropriate devote as much space as possible to rhododendrons, azaleas, heathers, and border plants, which are generally hardy and undemanding.
- Reduce or avoid areas devoted exclusively to annuals, especially beds of geometrical shapes where high time and energy commitment is essential.
- During hot, dry August days, avoid deep cultivation in your flower-beds. Loosening the soil under these conditions reduces water uptake by increasing loss of soil water and damaging surface roots. Plants often look much worse after cultivation than before.
- The fork is a more efficient tool than the spade, being more effective at circulating air throughout the soil, whether dry or wet. In addition, a fork is more likely to penetrate hardened ground than the spade.
- Compost or peat should be scattered over the surface and worked into the ground to a few centimetres deep. It should not be buried deep down where its benefits will be lost.
- Weeding a damp garden is much easier than weeding when the ground is dry – the entire root pulls out instead of breaking off.

- Stretch and do warm-up exercises before weeding. This helps with sore muscles and body parts the next day.
- May and September are the main months for combating the growth of weeds. You can expect weeds to be more prevalent in September.

SECTION 13

# Composting

Composting is a microbial process that converts plant materials such as grass clippings, garden refuse, and leaves into a more usable organic soil or mulch. In its final state of decomposition, it is referred to as humus. Gardeners have used compost for centuries to increase soil organic matter, and to supply some of the essential nutrients for plant growth. Well-decomposed, earthy composts are good soil improvers. They make the soil easier to work, and create a better medium for plant growth. You can mix compost into your soil before you plant a garden, lawn, perennial bed, or cover crop.

## THE SLOW METHOD

Well-rotted, home-made compost is an easy and convenient way to improve the soil, and saves you the trouble of bagging up garden and kitchen vegetable waste. It is often the best method for people who do not have the time to tend a hot compost heap. Simply mix non-woody garden waste into a heap and let it sit for a year or so. Micro-organisms, insects, earthworms, and other decomposers will slowly break down the wastes. A mixture of energy materials and bulking agents provides the best food source and environment for decomposition.

Add fresh waste to the compost heap by opening the heap, placing fresh waste into the centre, and covering it. This helps aerate the heap, and also buries the fresh waste so that it doesn't attract pests.

Fruit and vegetable waste is particularly appealing to pests, such as flies and rats. To avoid pests, bury these wastes within the heap. If, despite this, pests are still a problem, you may need to screen the heap or keep vegetable waste out.

You also can bury vegetable waste directly in your garden. Dig a hole or a trench about a foot deep, add a few centimetres of vegetable waste, mix it with the soil, and refill the trench with soil. Another way to avoid pests is to compost vegetable waste in a worm bin.

Slow composting does not produce the heat needed to kill many weed seeds. It is best to pull and compost weeds before they go to seed. If you put seeds in the compost heap, be prepared for more weeding.

## THE FAST METHOD

Good garden compost results if you create and maintain a balance of air, moisture, and energy for the compost micro-organisms. They will produce hot compost that will break down quickly and kill off many weed seeds and disease organisms. Making hot compost takes extra effort, but it produces a high-quality product quickly. One method for making hot compost is described below.

### Building the compost

Simply choose a site in the garden that is accessible but well screened, dry and free draining. It should not be anywhere too damp or shaded or the compost will not rot down correctly. You do not need a bin or other container to make compost. Some people prefer containers because they look neater, or because it is easier to shield them from pests.

Containers can be simple or fancy. Make them from materials such as old pallets, timber, mesh fencing, or concrete blocks. For hot compost, each bin should be about 1 cubic metre in size. Compost heaps should be ideally situated out of direct sunlight and cold winds. Avid gardeners often have three bins: two for turning, and one for curing compost.

Step 1: Collect enough material to make a heap at least 1 cubic metre in volume (an open heap 1.5 metres wide at the base by 1 metre high holds about a cubic metre). You need roughly two parts bulking agent to one part energy material. Chop, shred, mow, or crush coarse materials so they will break down faster.

Step 2: Start the heap by adding a level layer of vegetable waste about 50cm deep, mixing with a fork. Sprinkle the surface with a compost activator. Add a 5cm layer of soil, and then continue to add your garden refuse and kitchen vegetable waste to the heap. Lightly tread down the heap whenever you add to it, to remove air pockets that hinder decomposition.

Keep a waterproof lid on the heap at all times to prevent heat escaping and to stop rain getting in.

### Turning the compost

Use a fork to turn the heap weekly, and add water when needed. Turning gets air into the centre of the heap and speeds the biological decay. Turning also mixes material from the outside of the heap into the hot centre.

### Curing phase

After initial mixing, a regularly turned heap usually stays hot (50°C to 65°C) for a month to several weeks. The heap will shrink to about half its original volume during the hot phase. It then needs to sit for one or two months to cure. Temperatures during curing are 27°C to 43°C. The compost is ready to use when at least two months have passed since initial mixing, the heap no longer heats when turned, and the material looks dark and crumbly.

Curing affects the availability of nitrogen and the microbial activity of the compost. Uncured compost may harm some plants. This is most likely when compost is used in potting soil or to start seeds. Curing is less critical when small amounts of compost are worked into the soil.

## COMPOSTING AND THE ENVIRONMENT

Garden composting reduces the flow of wastes to landfill sites, and produces valuable organic matter for the soil at the same time. Composting does all this using a process fuelled by the solar energy captured in plant tissue. These benefits are the same whether you compost in carefully tended hot heaps, or in neglected slow heaps. Garden composting is a simple, yet important way to improve the environment.

Use pine bark chips to keep moisture in areas that are subjected to a lot of sunlight. This helps to keep the need for watering down, especially when there are water restrictions in your area for the summer months.

Wood shavings, as used for horse stalls, work well as mulch. Cover the area, and then use normal mulch to cover. This method holds moisture, breaks down extremely well, and goes a long way.

Always spread your mulch right over everything and mix with the topsoil about once a week with a garden claw to prevent weeds.

## TIPS

### 1. How can I use compost?

Compost can be used to enrich the garden, to improve the soil around trees and shrubs, as a soil improver for house-plants, and when screened, as part of a seed-starting mix or lawn top-dressing.

### 2. What if my hot compost isn't hot?

If the heap is dry, it needs more moisture.

If the heap is mostly woody garden refuse, it needs more nitrogen. Add more softer plant material or nitrogen fertiliser.

If the heap is too wet, add more woody garden refuse. Make sure the cover is waterproof or build a larger heap.
If the heap has a foul smell, it needs more air and less water. Try turning the heap more often or adding more woody garden refuse.
If the heap is too small, it will not hold the heat.
If it is cold outside, try building a larger heap to hold the heat.

Sometimes you may have several problems to overcome. If you cannot get the heap to heat, all is not lost, because the heap will still break down by the slow method.

### 3. Can I dispose of diseased plants and weeds in my compost?

If you are composting by the slow method keep diseased plants and seed-heads of weeds out of your compost heap. For any compost, avoid coarse, woody materials because they break down slowly and make the heap hard to turn.

### 4. Can I use farmyard manure in my compost?

If you use fresh manure in a slow compost heap or directly in your garden, a small risk exists that disease-causing pathogens will contaminate garden vegetables. To reduce the risk of disease, allow at least 60 days between applying manure and harvesting any vegetables that will be eaten without cooking. The risk is greatest for root crops such as carrots and radishes, or leaf crops, like lettuce, where the edible part touches the soil. Careful washing or peeling will remove most of the pathogens responsible for disease. Thorough cooking is even more effective at killing pathogens on garden crops.

### 5. Can I dispose of my dog and cat faeces on the compost heap?

It is best to keep dog, cat, and pig manure out of your compost heap and garden. Some of the parasites that are found in these manures may survive the composting process and remain infectious for people.

### 6. Are herbicides harmful in compost?

Some people are concerned that herbicides in compost can harm plants. Most herbicides in home compost heaps come from lawn clippings. The warm temperatures in a compost heap accelerate herbicide breakdown to non-toxic compounds. Binding with organic matter in the compost also inactivates herbicides. Breakdown and binding reduce the risk of herbicide damage.

If you have recently treated your lawn with a herbicide, return treated grass clippings to the lawn rather than composting them. Some lawn herbicides may persist in the soil for six to eight months. However, composting accelerates the degradation process. If treated grass clippings are composted for at least one year, pesticide residue should not be a problem when the compost is used in the garden or landscape.

### 7. Is it true that banana skins are good for the compost heap?

Keep banana skins and add to your garden's compost heap. Banana skins are a rich source of phosphorous and potassium.

### 8. Is it necessary to add lime (calcium) to the compost heap?

Most finished compost will have a near neutral pH without the addition of lime. However, the bacteria in your compost heap needs nitrogen to flourish and do its job of breaking down the waste produce, but it also increases the acidity of the compost. To counteract the increase in acidity, sprinkle a very small amount of lime on the surface. Too much lime may cause a loss of nitrogen from the heap, so sprinkle sulphate of ammonia at alternate depths of 50cm when building up your compost. In this way, the lime will reduce the acidity, and the sulphate of ammonia will give the bacteria the nitrogen it needs. Make sure that the lime and sulphate of ammonia don't come into contact with each other.

**9. Can I use seaweed in my compost?**
Seaweed is especially good in composts. It is a valuable source of trace elements such as iodine.

**10. What is mulching?**
When compost is applied to the soil surface to help control weeds, conserve water, or protect the soil from erosion, it is known as mulching. The best time to mulch is in early summer, after plants are established and the soil has warmed. Later, it can be dug into the soil. When using it as a mulch for perennial plantings, choose compost made from woody garden refuse, because it decomposes slowly, resists compaction, and slows weed establishment.

**11. Does compost have any value as a fertiliser?**
Yes, because decomposed materials have some nitrogen, phosphorous and potassium content even though in small amounts. The addition of garden fertilisers helps to speed up decomposition and supplies some of the nutrients as well.

**12. Can I use compost as a replacement for commercial fertilisers?**
It can be used as a source of nutrients; however, there are not enough nutrients present in the compost to supply the needs of vegetable crops and ornamental plants. The amount of nutrients in compost depends on the materials that have been placed in the compost.

**13. What do I do with composted particles that are not fully decomposed?**
In ordinary composting any particles that are too large can be forked or screened out, broken up and put back in the compost heap when

necessary. If the material is to be used on lawns or flower gardens, it can be screened after composting through a 1 cm or smaller screen to give it a better appearance and to make it easier to apply and work into the soil.

**14. What are the best materials for composting?**
Most plant material can be used for composting. Leaves are perhaps the best materials because of their availability and organic content; however, other types of organic materials such as grass clippings, vegetable refuse, small tree limbs and shrub trimmings, tea bags, and rotted sawdust are considered good composting materials. Do not compost diseased plants, weeds with seeds, or invasive weeds; avoid composting faeces, meat products, or materials contaminated with chemicals.

**15. Is it necessary to shred materials for the compost heap?**
The finer the material is that goes into the compost heap the quicker and more thorough the decomposition.

**16. Can I use my rotary mower to shred materials?**
Yes, it works best on dry materials that are not too woody. For example, leaves can be shredded effectively by a rotary mower. It is best to use it on a hard, level surface.

**17. Do compost heaps need turning?**
Yes, turn the heap to supply more oxygen for the microbe population and to shift material on the edge of the pile to the centre where it, too, will be decomposed.

**18. How do you know when to turn the compost?**
If you are making hot compost, turn the heap when the internal temperature decreases below 38°C.

**19. When is compost ready to use?**
When the heap returns to normal temperature and the organic material crumbles easily. At this point, you should not be able to recognise the material that you put in the original heap. The composting process in the average heap takes about six to eight months, though an ideally mixed and tended heap may take less than two months to become compost.

**20. How do you know when compost is finished?**
When it has become dark, loose and crumbly; and if in a hot pile, when it doesn't reheat upon turning. Sift out undecomposed materials and place back in the compost heap.

**21. Do compost heaps normally have an offensive odour?**
Not if composting is done properly, (i.e., provided good aeration and moisture for rapid decomposition are present). If animal manures are used, some odour may be detectable in the beginning but will dissipate as the process accelerates.

**22. Should I get rid of the earwigs that invade my compost heap?**
Earwigs are rarely a serious threat to crops and they can be an aid to the composting process as scavengers. They prefer cooler piles.

**23. Can shredded newspaper be composted?**
Yes. The inks used today are generally non-toxic.

**24. How are harmful weeds composted?**
Plants that propagate vegetatively should be very thoroughly dried in the sun and then used as a compost ingredient. Alternatively, they should be composted alone and covered with black plastic to sit for as long as two years. A thorough composting in a hot system should kill most weed seeds.

**25. Can bones and meat scraps be composted?**
Yes, but there is too much potential for pest problems, so they are not recommended composting materials.

**26. Can wood ashes be added to the compost pile?**
Yes, but in very small quantities.

**27. Can sod be composted?**
Yes, stacked in a pile, grass side down, kept moist and covered with black plastic. It can take up to two years to fully compost.

**28. Do slugs retard the composting process?**
They are not a problem for the composting process – they actually contribute to the process by feeding on decaying and fresh wastes. Their proximity to the garden can, of course, be a problem.

**29. Can citrus fruit skin be composted?**
Yes. With citrus, it is best to chop the rinds as much as possible to aid decomposition. Compost them like other food wastes.

**30. Should diseased materials be used to make compost?**
As a general rule, it would be best not to compost diseased plant materials because of the chance of reinfecting your garden.

Section 14

# Insects, Pests And Remedies

- Soot deters insects, especially the onion gnat and turnip fly. Sprinkle liberally around onion and turnip plants. Another excellent treatment for the little pests is nicotine or tar oil.
- To deter fruit flies from decimating your apple trees, coat a red ball with molasses. Hang the ball in the tree to attract the flies where they will become stuck to it.
- Plant French or African marigolds alongside tomatoes, and lettuce in the greenhouse. This is an environmentally-friendly alternative way to control greenfly, blackfly and whitefly which do not like the aroma of this flower. Not only do you get a safe crop but you also have additional flowers for your home.
- To catch earwigs – make small holes in the side of a plastic container, pour a small amount of beer and cover. You will be surprised at how many earwigs you can catch.
- Herbs are nature's insecticides, so be sure to include a variety of them in your garden.
- Plant basil near tomatoes, as it will repel worms and flies.
- For pest control in your water-garden, collect frogs' spawn and place it in your pond.
- If you have a problem with herons stealing your fish, you may like to place a stone heron at the edge of your pond – real herons won't come to the pond so your fish are safe.
- To help control algae in your water-garden, submerge a nylon bag filled with barley hay in the water.

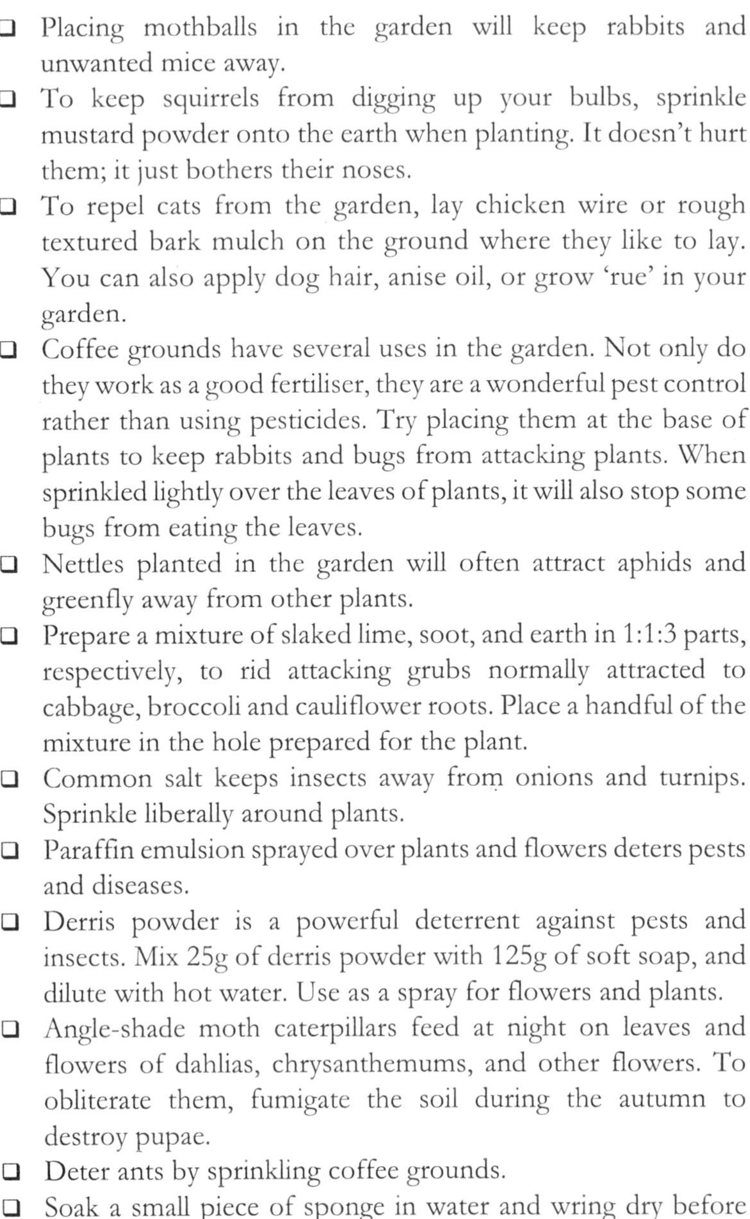

- Placing mothballs in the garden will keep rabbits and unwanted mice away.
- To keep squirrels from digging up your bulbs, sprinkle mustard powder onto the earth when planting. It doesn't hurt them; it just bothers their noses.
- To repel cats from the garden, lay chicken wire or rough textured bark mulch on the ground where they like to lay. You can also apply dog hair, anise oil, or grow 'rue' in your garden.
- Coffee grounds have several uses in the garden. Not only do they work as a good fertiliser, they are a wonderful pest control rather than using pesticides. Try placing them at the base of plants to keep rabbits and bugs from attacking plants. When sprinkled lightly over the leaves of plants, it will also stop some bugs from eating the leaves.
- Nettles planted in the garden will often attract aphids and greenfly away from other plants.
- Prepare a mixture of slaked lime, soot, and earth in 1:1:3 parts, respectively, to rid attacking grubs normally attracted to cabbage, broccoli and cauliflower roots. Place a handful of the mixture in the hole prepared for the plant.
- Common salt keeps insects away from onions and turnips. Sprinkle liberally around plants.
- Paraffin emulsion sprayed over plants and flowers deters pests and diseases.
- Derris powder is a powerful deterrent against pests and insects. Mix 25g of derris powder with 125g of soft soap, and dilute with hot water. Use as a spray for flowers and plants.
- Angle-shade moth caterpillars feed at night on leaves and flowers of dahlias, chrysanthemums, and other flowers. To obliterate them, fumigate the soil during the autumn to destroy pupae.
- Deter ants by sprinkling coffee grounds.
- Soak a small piece of sponge in water and wring dry before

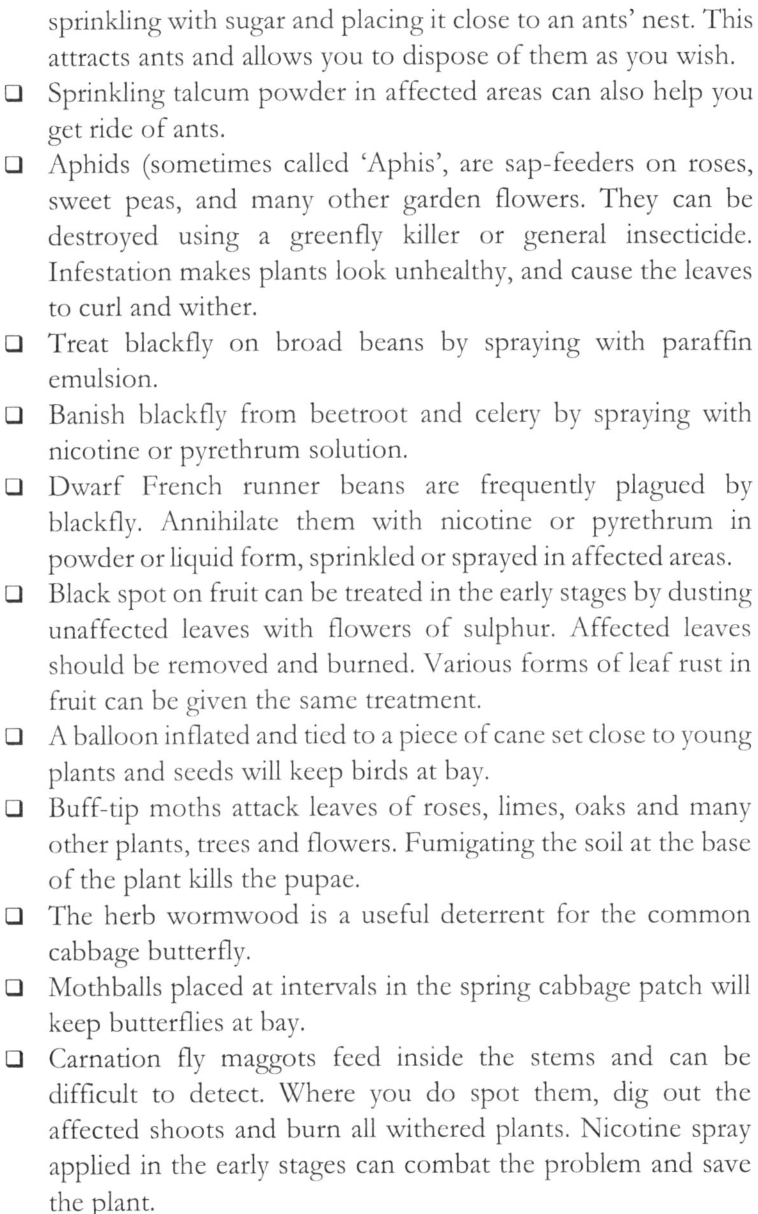

sprinkling with sugar and placing it close to an ants' nest. This attracts ants and allows you to dispose of them as you wish.

- Sprinkling talcum powder in affected areas can also help you get ride of ants.
- Aphids (sometimes called 'Aphis', are sap-feeders on roses, sweet peas, and many other garden flowers. They can be destroyed using a greenfly killer or general insecticide. Infestation makes plants look unhealthy, and cause the leaves to curl and wither.
- Treat blackfly on broad beans by spraying with paraffin emulsion.
- Banish blackfly from beetroot and celery by spraying with nicotine or pyrethrum solution.
- Dwarf French runner beans are frequently plagued by blackfly. Annihilate them with nicotine or pyrethrum in powder or liquid form, sprinkled or sprayed in affected areas.
- Black spot on fruit can be treated in the early stages by dusting unaffected leaves with flowers of sulphur. Affected leaves should be removed and burned. Various forms of leaf rust in fruit can be given the same treatment.
- A balloon inflated and tied to a piece of cane set close to young plants and seeds will keep birds at bay.
- Buff-tip moths attack leaves of roses, limes, oaks and many other plants, trees and flowers. Fumigating the soil at the base of the plant kills the pupae.
- The herb wormwood is a useful deterrent for the common cabbage butterfly.
- Mothballs placed at intervals in the spring cabbage patch will keep butterflies at bay.
- Carnation fly maggots feed inside the stems and can be difficult to detect. Where you do spot them, dig out the affected shoots and burn all withered plants. Nicotine spray applied in the early stages can combat the problem and save the plant.

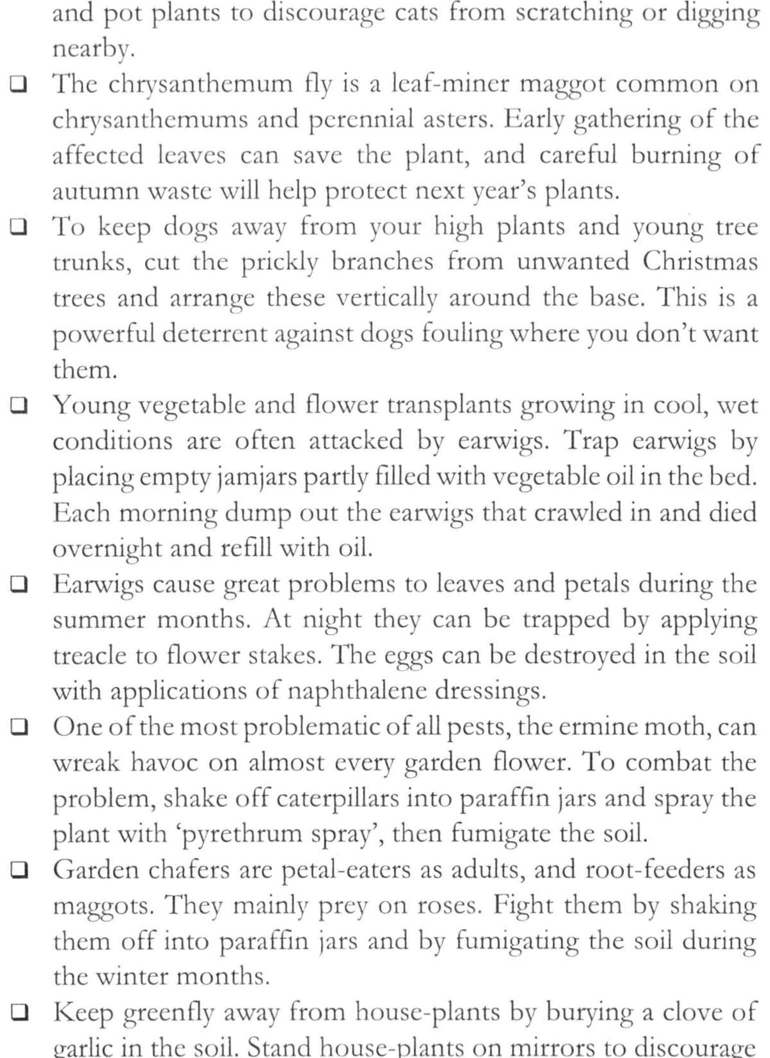

- Sprinkle a few crushed mothballs around your flower-beds and pot plants to discourage cats from scratching or digging nearby.
- The chrysanthemum fly is a leaf-miner maggot common on chrysanthemums and perennial asters. Early gathering of the affected leaves can save the plant, and careful burning of autumn waste will help protect next year's plants.
- To keep dogs away from your high plants and young tree trunks, cut the prickly branches from unwanted Christmas trees and arrange these vertically around the base. This is a powerful deterrent against dogs fouling where you don't want them.
- Young vegetable and flower transplants growing in cool, wet conditions are often attacked by earwigs. Trap earwigs by placing empty jamjars partly filled with vegetable oil in the bed. Each morning dump out the earwigs that crawled in and died overnight and refill with oil.
- Earwigs cause great problems to leaves and petals during the summer months. At night they can be trapped by applying treacle to flower stakes. The eggs can be destroyed in the soil with applications of naphthalene dressings.
- One of the most problematic of all pests, the ermine moth, can wreak havoc on almost every garden flower. To combat the problem, shake off caterpillars into paraffin jars and spray the plant with 'pyrethrum spray', then fumigate the soil.
- Garden chafers are petal-eaters as adults, and root-feeders as maggots. They mainly prey on roses. Fight them by shaking them off into paraffin jars and by fumigating the soil during the winter months.
- Keep greenfly away from house-plants by burying a clove of garlic in the soil. Stand house-plants on mirrors to discourage greenfly.
- Remove green fungi from cement paths and patios by soaking with bleach diluted in water, and then scrubbing with a brush.

- Green-veined butterflies are injurious to mignonette, wallflower, tropaeolum, and other plants. They can be killed with pyrethrum spray and by seeking and collecting chrysalides from fences.
- The holly miner causes blisters on holly, laburnum and lilac leaves. Combat the problem by gathering and burning all affected foliage during the spring and autumn months.
- Leather-jackets are root-feeders, and are attracted to most plants. Soil fumigation in winter is essential. Destruction of 'Daddy Long Legs' in autumn is vital.
- The mealy bug is a sap-feeder attracted to many greenhouse plants. Guard against them by spraying plants with soft soap and paraffin in early summer.
- To prevent mildew, dissolve a handful of ordinary soda in boiling water and leave to cool. Use as a spray for roses.
- Narcissus fly maggots burrow into bulbs during autumn and winter. Digging and fumigation kills wandering grubs. Burn all affected bulbs to stop the problem spreading to other plants.
- Potatoes and carrots attract millipedes. Keep them at bay by burying a few potatoes or carrots in the ground at spots well away from the plants you want to deter them from. You can place slices of either vegetable on a stick buried slightly below the ground. Remove the stick daily and examine it for pests.
- Scare off moles and rabbits by setting empty bottles into the ground, leaving just the rim exposed. The whistling sound made by the wind as it blows over the bottles is a powerful deterrent for moles.
- If moles are the pests you want to get rid of, follow the same practice using the bottles, but keep adding castor oil to the rim of the bottles. Moles hate the smell of castor oil.
- Parsnip grubs found burrowing into parsnip leaves can be treated by spraying with nicotine and pyrethrum solution.

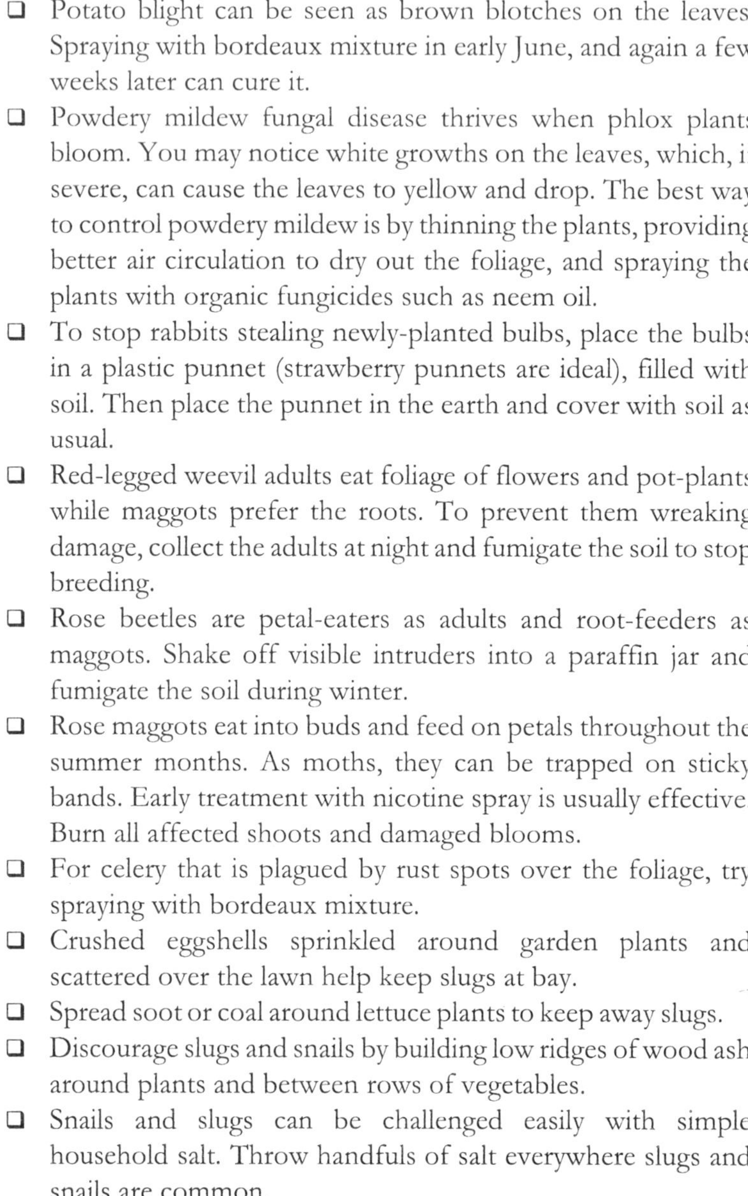

- ❑ Potato blight can be seen as brown blotches on the leaves. Spraying with bordeaux mixture in early June, and again a few weeks later can cure it.
- ❑ Powdery mildew fungal disease thrives when phlox plants bloom. You may notice white growths on the leaves, which, if severe, can cause the leaves to yellow and drop. The best way to control powdery mildew is by thinning the plants, providing better air circulation to dry out the foliage, and spraying the plants with organic fungicides such as neem oil.
- ❑ To stop rabbits stealing newly-planted bulbs, place the bulbs in a plastic punnet (strawberry punnets are ideal), filled with soil. Then place the punnet in the earth and cover with soil as usual.
- ❑ Red-legged weevil adults eat foliage of flowers and pot-plants while maggots prefer the roots. To prevent them wreaking damage, collect the adults at night and fumigate the soil to stop breeding.
- ❑ Rose beetles are petal-eaters as adults and root-feeders as maggots. Shake off visible intruders into a paraffin jar and fumigate the soil during winter.
- ❑ Rose maggots eat into buds and feed on petals throughout the summer months. As moths, they can be trapped on sticky bands. Early treatment with nicotine spray is usually effective. Burn all affected shoots and damaged blooms.
- ❑ For celery that is plagued by rust spots over the foliage, try spraying with bordeaux mixture.
- ❑ Crushed eggshells sprinkled around garden plants and scattered over the lawn help keep slugs at bay.
- ❑ Spread soot or coal around lettuce plants to keep away slugs.
- ❑ Discourage slugs and snails by building low ridges of wood ash around plants and between rows of vegetables.
- ❑ Snails and slugs can be challenged easily with simple household salt. Throw handfuls of salt everywhere slugs and snails are common.

- Sprinkle salt on paths and crevices to remove weeds and grass.
- Attract slugs and snails by leaving fresh orange peel lying in affected areas. Both are attracted to the white side where they will gather and make collecting easy.
- A dish of beer will attract slugs, beetles, and snails. Add a little water and some sugar to the beer to make it extra inviting.
- Dwarf French runner beans are common haunts of tiny red spiders that can be removed with an early evening spray of clear water over affected areas.
- The swallowtail moth is a stick caterpillar known to favour ivy, elder, honeysuckle, roses, forget-me-not, and various shrubs. Shaking them off into a jar of paraffin and gathering cocoons during the spring can kill it.
- Thrips are sap-feeders on sweet peas, chrysanthemums, and many other flowers. Fumigation of the soil in autumn and spring is highly effective. Early spraying with nicotine can save affected plants.
- If your tomato fruits have a black, rotted spot on the blossom end (the end away from the plant), then it's likely they have blossom-end rot. This condition is caused by fluctuating soil moisture conditions, which create a calcium deficiency in the fruit. The cell walls break down, and the fruit rots. To prevent this condition, mulch the plants and water them regularly.
- Tomato blight can be seen as green and black spots on tomato leaves. Spraying with bordeaux mixture can treat it.
- There are a number of fungi that cause strawberries to rot. One of the most common ones is grey mould. Both young and ripening fruits develop a cottony-white to grey-coloured fuzzy growth on the fruit surface, which eventually causes the fruit to rot. To lessen the damage, mulch with meadow hay to prevent spores from splashing on the fruits. Destroy infected fruits as soon as they are noticed.
- To prevent grey mould on strawberries, plant in raised beds, spacing plants 30 to 45cm apart, and avoid overhead watering.

- For young cabbage plants that are affected by turnip flies, dust the area with soot, derris, or nicotine powder.
- Waved umber moths are leaf-eaters on roses and privets. Capture the adults by shaking off into a paraffin jar and carefully fumigate soil at the base.
- Deter weevils on broad bean seedlings by sprinkling soot or derris powder over the foliage.

# Index

## Q



## R



## S

## T



## V



## W